An Analysis of

Plato's

Symposium

Richard Ellis
with
Simon Ravenscroft

Published by Macat International Ltd
24:13 Coda Centre, 189 Munster Road, London SW6 6AW.

Distributed exclusively by Routledge
2 Park Square, Milton Park, Abingdon, Oxon OX14 4RN
711 Third Avenue, New York, NY 10017, USA

Routledge is an imprint of the Taylor & Francis Group, an informa business

www.macat.com
info@macat.com

Cataloguing in Publication Data
A catalogue record for this book is available from the British Library.
Library of Congress Cataloguing-in-Publication Data is available upon request.
Cover illustration: Etienne Gilfillan

ISBN 978-1-912303-12-0 (hardback)
ISBN 978-1-912127-66-5 (paperback)
ISBN 978-1-912282-00-5 (e-book)

Notice
The information in this book is designed to orientate readers of the work under analysis,
to elucidate and contextualise its key ideas and themes, and to aid in the development
of critical thinking skills. It is not meant to be used, nor should it be used, as a
substitute for original thinking or in place of original writing or research. References and
notes are provided for informational purposes and their presence does not constitute
endorsement of the information or opinions therein. This book is presented solely for
educational purposes. It is sold on the understanding that the publisher is not engaged
to provide any scholarly advice. The publisher has made every effort to ensure that
this book is accurate and up-to-date, but makes no warranties or representations with
regard to the completeness or reliability of the information it contains. The information
and the opinions provided herein are not guaranteed or warranted to produce particular
results and may not be suitable for students of every ability. The publisher shall not be
liable for any loss, damage or disruption arising from any errors or omissions, or from
the use of this book, including, but not limited to, special, incidental, consequential or
other damages caused, or alleged to have been caused, directly or indirectly, by the
information contained within.

CONTENTS

THE MACAT LIBRARY

The Macat Library is a series of unique academic explorations of seminal works in the humanities and social sciences – books and papers that have had a significant and widely recognised impact on their disciplines. It has been created to serve as much more than just a summary of what lies between the covers of a great book. It illuminates and explores the influences on, ideas of, and impact of that book. Our goal is to offer a learning resource that encourages critical thinking and fosters a better, deeper understanding of important ideas.

Each publication is divided into three Sections: Influences, Ideas, and Impact. Each Section has four Modules. These explore every important facet of the work, and the responses to it.

This Section-Module structure makes a Macat Library book easy to use, but it has another important feature. Because each Macat book is written to the same format, it is possible (and encouraged!) to cross-reference multiple Macat books along the same lines of inquiry or research. This allows the reader to open up interesting interdisciplinary pathways.

To further aid your reading, lists of glossary terms and people mentioned are included at the end of this book (these are indicated by an asterisk [*] throughout) – as well as a list of works cited.

Macat has worked with the University of Cambridge to identify the elements of critical thinking and understand the ways in which six different skills combine to enable effective thinking.
Three allow us to fully understand a problem; three more give us the tools to solve it. Together, these six skills make up the **PACIER** model of critical thinking. They are:

ANALYSIS – understanding how an argument is built
EVALUATION – exploring the strengths and weaknesses of an argument
INTERPRETATION – understanding issues of meaning

CREATIVE THINKING – coming up with new ideas and fresh connections
PROBLEM-SOLVING – producing strong solutions
REASONING – creating strong arguments

To find out more, visit **WWW.MACAT.COM.**

CRITICAL THINKING AND *SYMPOSIUM*

Primary critical thinking skill: REASONING
Secondary critical thinking skill: EVALUATION

Plato's *Symposium*, composed in the early fourth century BC, demonstrates just how powerful the skills of reasoning and evaluation can be.

Known to philosophers for its seminal discussion of the relationship of love to knowledge, *Symposium* is also a classic text that shows the critical thinking skills that define Plato's whole body of work in action. Reasoning is the skill of producing arguments and presenting a persuasive case for one's point of view; evaluation is about judging the strength of arguments, their relevance and their acceptability. Plato's philosophical technique of dialogue is the perfect frame for these two skills. Staging a fictional debate between characters (wealthy Athenians at a dinner party) who must respond in turn to each others' arguments and points of view means that, at every stage, Plato evaluates the previous argument, assesses its strength and relevance, and then proceeds (through the next character) to reason out a new argument in response.

Exerting unparalleled influence on the techniques of philosophical thought, Plato's use of dialogue is a supreme example of these two crucial critical thinking skills.

ABOUT THE AUTHOR OF THE ORIGINAL WORK

Plato was born in Athens—then the intellectual center of the ancient world—around 429 b.c.e. Regarded as the most influential philosopher in the Western tradition of political philosophy, metaphysics, and ethics, Plato was a follower of the philosopher Socrates and teacher of the philosopher Aristotle. The founder of the famous Academy—an important center of learning just outside Athens—Plato died around 347 b.c.e.

ABOUT THE AUTHORS OF THE ANALYSIS

Dr Richard Ellis is a Lecturer in the Department of Classics at the University of California Los Angeles. His research interests include all areas of ancient Greek philosophy, with a specialisation in the Pre-Socratics, as well as the intersections between early Greek philosophy and literature and the philosophy of the 17th century British writer John Locke.

Dr Simon Ravenscroft is research fellow at the Von Hügel Institue for for Critical Catholic Enquiry at the University of Cambridge. His research interests sit at the intersection of theology, philosophy, literature, and political and social theory. His doctoral dissertation was on the philosophical and theological underpinnings of the social theory of the radical social theorist Ivan Illich.

ABOUT MACAT

GREAT WORKS FOR CRITICAL THINKING

Macat is focused on making the ideas of the world's great thinkers accessible and comprehensible to everybody, everywhere, in ways that promote the development of enhanced critical thinking skills.

It works with leading academics from the world's top universities to produce new analyses that focus on the ideas and the impact of the most influential works ever written across a wide variety of academic disciplines. Each of the works that sit at the heart of its growing library is an enduring example of great thinking. But by setting them in context – and looking at the influences that shaped their authors, as well as the responses they provoked – Macat encourages readers to look at these classics and game-changers with fresh eyes. Readers learn to think, engage and challenge their ideas, rather than simply accepting them.

'Macat offers an amazing first-of-its-kind tool for interdisciplinary learning and research. Its focus on works that transformed their disciplines and its rigorous approach, drawing on the world's leading experts and educational institutions, opens up a world-class education to anyone.'

Andreas Schleicher
Director for Education and Skills, Organisation for Economic Co-operation and Development

'Macat is taking on some of the major challenges in university education … They have drawn together a strong team of active academics who are producing teaching materials that are novel in the breadth of their approach.'

Prof Lord Broers,
former Vice-Chancellor of the University of Cambridge

'The Macat vision is exceptionally exciting. It focuses upon new modes of learning which analyse and explain seminal texts which have profoundly influenced world thinking and so social and economic development. It promotes the kind of critical thinking which is essential for any society and economy. This is the learning of the future.'

Rt Hon Charles Clarke, former UK Secretary of State for Education

'The Macat analyses provide immediate access to the critical conversation surrounding the books that have shaped their respective discipline, which will make them an invaluable resource to all of those, students and teachers, working in the field.'

Professor William Tronzo, University of California at San Diego

WAYS IN TO THE TEXT

KEY POINTS

- Plato was a Greek philosopher of the fifth to the fourth century b.c.e. He is one of the fathers of Western philosophy.
- *Symposium* uses a fictional dialogue to explore the relationship between erotic desire and virtue.
- The text, innovative in both style and philosophy, has influenced thinking about love, desire, and virtue for more than two thousand years.

Who was Plato?

The Greek philosopher Plato, a disciple of Socrates,* is one of the most famous and influential philosophers in any tradition. Although precise dates are difficult to establish, he is thought to have lived between about 425 and 348 b.c.e. He worked in the Greek city-state of Athens, where he established the philosophical school known as the Academy,* often taken to be the first academic institution of its kind in the Western world. In the period when Plato wrote and taught, Athens was the intellectual and cultural center of the classical world—a hub for philosophical debate and intellectual exchange.

Though some are of doubtful authenticity, Plato is the author of over 30 surviving philosophical dialogues, including *Symposium*, and a number of letters, known as "epistles." The dialogues take the form of philosophical debates between various figures of the day, the philosopher Socrates among them. They address matters such as the life of virtue and what constitutes wisdom (ethics), the ideals of governance and the state (politics), the character of human knowledge and the pursuit of truth (epistemology),* and the fundamental structures of reality (metaphysics).*

After his death, Plato's ideas continued to be discussed at the Academy and other philosophical schools in Athens and subsequently spread acreoss ancient Mediterranean cultures and beyond. Along with his student Aristotle,* Plato laid many of the foundations of Western philosophy and is considered one of the fathers of the Western philosophical tradition. His ideas have been absorbed into the intellectual culture of the West, just as they have influenced thinkers from other cultures, such as medieval Islamic philosophers like Alfarabi. They continue to have a great influence today.

What Does *Symposium* Say?

Symposium takes the form of a fictional dialogue between Athens's famous talkers, thinkers, and writers as they discuss matters of love and virtue. The text is structured as a series of speeches at a "symposium," a kind of dinner party at which men of high status would enjoy both material, bodily pleasures (through food, drink, and sex) and the more refined pleasures of the mind (through intellectual discussion). Each of the speeches is framed as being "in praise of Eros"*—the Greek term for the form of love associated with sexual desire and the root of the modern English word "erotic."

The fundamental question that *Symposium* addresses is the role of erotic desire in the philosophical pursuit of wisdom, virtue, and happiness. Specifically, it considers whether Eros is beneficial to the production of philosophy and to the living of an ethical life. Although the text takes the form of an open-ended conversation in which no speech reaches a definite conclusion (which means the dialogue offers many interpretations), we can be safe in understanding that Plato presents erotic desire, as related to philosophy and the virtuous life, in a positive way. This is made especially clear in the words Plato puts in the mouth of his former teacher, Socrates.

Erotic desire for beautiful, material things such as the human body can lead (says Plato's Socrates) to desire and love for higher and more refined forms of beauty such as the beauty of knowledge, virtue, and wisdom. Indeed, Eros should eventually lead us to the contemplation of beauty itself—the final goal of philosophy. The passage describing this journey, referred to as the Ascent to Beauty,* is one of the most famous in the Western tradition. Ultimately, Eros is presented as contributing in crucial ways both to the happiness and well-being of the individual and to the welfare of the community as a whole.

It is no surprise that *Symposium,* having proved to be one of Plato's most influential works, has had a significant impact on later writers and thinkers in two specific respects.

The first is through its literary originality. In describing a fictional dinner party where a philosophical debate is conducted in a light-hearted and often comic fashion, Plato created a type of philosophical literature with many subsequent imitators.[1]

The second is through an analysis of love and erotic desire, and of their relation to virtue and ethics, that has shaped almost every following discussion of any importance on this subject. Plato's student Aristotle, for example, places less emphasis on Eros in his *Nicomachean Ethics.* The difference between Plato's and Aristotle's texts continues to structure many debates around the "ideal" form of love, even in the present day.

Finally, in a broader sense, *Symposium* is of crucial academic and cultural importance as a part of Plato's wider body of work (his corpus), given the general influence of his ideas on the intellectual life of the West, and on philosophy in particular.

Why Does *Symposium* Matter?

Symposium provides an introduction to one of the most influential writers in the history of human thought. In that context alone, its ideas would be worth consideration.

We generally share Plato's assumption that contemplation of *Symposium's* central themes—love, desire, virtue, wisdom, and happiness—is essential to address the issue of how a life should best be lived. Ancient philosophy is unlike much modern academic philosophy in that it explicitly and continually concerns itself with the question of the "good life;" indeed, in many ways ancient philosophy was understood to be a practice and a way of life in itself.[2] This is evident in *Symposium*, a text concerned with the ways in which desire—and especially erotic desire—can serve virtue and the pursuit of wisdom. Even today, *Symposium* offers us the possibility of reflection on the kinds of lives we might lead, and particularly on how we might think and act in relation to matters of desire and love.

The work's form is also significant. *Symposium's* complex structure, a long "conversation" in which ideas are never definitively resolved, does not provide the reader with easy answers to the questions it raises. For modern academic writing, this apparent lack of clarity would be regarded as a failing. In Plato's work, however, it is designed to help us realize that the pursuit of wisdom and truth is not necessarily a straightforward task. We cannot always find neat solutions to life's problems.

Symposium tells us that academic study is not simply a question of discovering answers or learning facts. It is about developing ways of thinking and communicating that are valuable in themselves—what Plato would have regarded as intellectual virtues. This is a lesson valuable to students of disciplines beyond philosophy.

Finally, in a more general sense, the influence of Plato, and *Symposium* in particular, on Western thought and culture is so profound that to study the text is to gain an understanding of the heritage on which modern culture is founded.

NOTES

1   Richard Hunter, *Plato's Symposium* (Oxford: Oxford University Press, 2004), 9–10, 126.

2   Pierre Hadot, *Philosophy as a Way of Life: Spiritual Exercises From Socrates to Foucault,* trans. Michael Chase (Oxford: Wiley-Blackwell, 1995), 49–70, 147–78.

SECTION 1
INFLUENCES

MODULE 1
THE AUTHOR AND THE
HISTORICAL CONTEXT

KEY POINTS

- *Symposium* gave rise to a new genre of philosophical literature and has informed debate on the themes of ethics, love, and desire ever since it was written.
- Plato was a student and follower of Socrates,* one of the key characters in *Symposium*.
- In ancient Greece, symposia were social events where both the bodily pleasures of food, drink, and sex and the intellectual pleasures of the mind were enjoyed.

Why Read this Text?

The philosophy of Plato has had an enormous impact on Western thought. But as much as *Symposium* has contributed to that impact, being one of the central texts of Plato's body of work (his corpus), it is also one of his most quirky, challenging, and difficult works.

The text is structured as a fictional dialogue between several of Plato's contemporaries at a "symposium" (a kind of dinner party), where the conversation reaches no definite conclusions. This is perhaps a somewhat complex literary form but one which is highly original in style and which gave rise to a whole new category of philosophical literature.[1]

The text's central themes consider the ways in which erotic desire might contribute positively to the pursuit of virtue and philosophical truth. Plato's reflections on this subject, in speeches given to the characters in the dialogue, have had an important influence on Western thought, from the classical philosophers of his own era such as

> ** Both the setting of this dialogue at a symposium, and the focus on the erotic relationships that typically took place at such an event, is a natural way in which to explore the ethics of desire in [ancient Greek] culture, since the context itself was one which attempted to make Eros* work towards certain cultural norms. **
>
> Frisbee C. C. Sheffield, *Plato's Symposium: The Ethics of Desire*

his student Aristotle,* to some of the most important Christian* theologians (those who study God) like St. Augustine.* This influence continues to be felt in the work of modern scholars in a wide variety of fields. Alongside Plato's discussions of similar subjects in his *Lysis* and *Phaedrus*, *Symposium* continues to be studied because of its literary originality, its philosophical merit, and its cultural impact across many centuries.

Author's Life

The philosopher Plato is thought to have been born in or near Athens around 425 B.C.E. to parents with illustrious ancestors. His father, Ariston, was related to a former king of Athens, while the family of his mother, Perictione, was linked to Solon,* an important Athenian lawgiver of the late sixth century B.C.E.[2] Plato grew up in Athens, a city where thinkers, poets, and philosophers congregated. His education was typical of an elite Athenian male. He learned letters (formal scholarship and literature) and wrestling in private schools before taking up creative activities such as painting and the composition of poetry, especially tragedies.[3]

In his youth Plato spent time talking and discussing with philosophers. It is recorded that he was influenced by a thinker who knew and understood the ideas of Heraclitus,* an older philosopher who believed that the nature and structure of the world was maintained through the dynamic action of change.[4] When he later encountered the philosopher Socrates, Plato quickly became a follower. Socrates remained the most important influence on Plato's life and philosophy, and features as one of the key characters in *Symposium*.

Like most Athenians, Plato followed a polytheistic* religion. This meant he believed in the existence of several gods and goddesses. Religious rituals were a part of both political and social life to the extent that modern scholars find it difficult to distinguish between religious identity and civic* identity in ancient Athens. In particular, it is worth bearing in mind Plato's exposure to mystery cults, in which political and religious forms of identity were intertwined, since revelation was reserved for a select group of initiates. The Eleusinian Mysteries* that took place near Athens, for example, provide a backdrop to *Symposium*'s presentation of the ritual ascent to the Form of Beauty.*[5] The philosopher is here depicted as progressing from desire for material things, such as beautiful bodies, to immaterial things, such as beautiful ideas, finally to a contemplation of beauty itself, in its eternal and unchanging form, beyond matter and time.

Author's Background

It is likely that Plato wrote *Symposium* in Athens, the main intellectual center of the ancient Greek world. Described as "the enlightened city *par excellence*,"[6] it was a place of great commercial, institutional, poetical, and philosophical energy where ideas were generated and presented to eager audiences in theaters, courtrooms, public assemblies, and in philosophical debates. Having founded his philosophical school, the Academy,* in Athens, Plato went on to contribute to the intellectually fertile environment that had made him.

The title of Plato's *Symposium* refers to the work's fictional setting: an all-male social gathering with drinking, dining, intellectual conversation, and other forms of entertainment that usually included paid performers, both musical and sexual. Throughout the ancient Greek world, a symposium was an event for men of high status. As an occasion where cultural values and ideas were enacted and transmitted from one generation to another, it represented more than a mere dinner party.[7] It stood, in effect, for an aristocratic "alternative society"[8] operating in parallel to the more democratic and open institutions of the Athenian city-state of the fifth century B.C.E. The title, therefore, does not merely name the setting for Plato's philosophical treatise,* it indicates the intellectual and cultural framework in which the work is positioned.

Although *Symposium* was written in approximately 380 B.C.E.,[9] it describes a fictional symposium held in 416 B.C.E. (that is, more than 30 years earlier). The "cast" includes several of the period's most important figures—the philosopher Socrates, the playwrights Aristophanes* and Agathon,* and the infamous young general Alcibiades,* whose actions after 416 B.C.E. played a pivotal role in the outcome of the Peloponnesian War* between Athens and Sparta.*[10]

From the perspective of the audience in 380 B.C.E., *Symposium* does not simply consider timeless philosophical questions about virtue and desire. It puts them in the mouths of historical characters who were of significance to the people of the day. It is especially worth noting the context provided by the execution of one of *Symposium*'s main characters, Socrates, in 399 B.C.E. Socrates had a hold on the Athenian imagination, and was an important figure in Plato's own life. The vivid picture *Symposium* paints of him would surely have made people think, if only implicitly, about the charges of which he was convicted: namely, corrupting the youth of Athens and impiety towards the gods of the state.[11]

NOTES

1   Richard Hunter, *Plato's Symposium* (Oxford: Oxford University Press, 2004), 9–10, 126.

2   W. K. C. Guthrie, *A History of Greek Philosophy,* vol. 4, *Plato: The Man and His Dialogues: Earlier Period* (Cambridge: Cambridge University Press, 1986), 10.

3   Guthrie, *History of Greek Philosophy,* vol. 4, 12–7.

4   Guthrie, *History of Greek Philosophy,* vol. 4, 33; Debra Nails, *The People of Plato: A Prosopography of Plato and Other Socratics* (Indianapolis: Hackett Publishing, 2002), 105–6.

5   Frisbee C. C. Sheffield, *Plato's Symposium: The Ethics of Desire* (Oxford: Oxford University Press, 2006), 219.

6   Steven Berg, *Eros and the Intoxications of Enlightenment: On Plato's Symposium* (Albany, NY: State University of New York Press, 2010), x.

7   Hunter, *Plato's Symposium,* 5–7.

8   Hunter, *Plato's Symposium*, 6.

9   K. Dover, "The Date of Plato's *Symposium,*" *Phronesis* 10 (1965): 2–20; Hunter, *Plato's Symposium*, 3.

10 Hunter, *Plato's Symposium,* 4–5.

11 Berg, *Eros and the Intoxications of Enlightenment,* x–xii.

MODULE 2
ACADEMIC CONTEXT

KEY POINTS

- Ancient Greek philosophy is concerned with fundamental questions about the nature of reality and the character of a good human life.

- At the time of *The Symposium*'s writing, Eros* (that is, the influence of love and sexual desire) was not considered fundamentally related to philosophy or the pursuit of the "good life."

- Plato questions commonly held views of the time by celebrating erotic desire as fundamental for philosophy and the virtuous life.

The Work In Its Context

In ancient Greece, the student of philosophy—a word that literally means "love of wisdom," from the Greek words *philia* and *sophos*—was someone engaged in the study of the fundamental structures of reality and the nature of the good and virtuous life. This included the school of Pythagoreanism,* which sought to describe the world as a coherent mathematical system. According to tradition, Plato is said to have spent time with Pythagorean philosophers in southern Italy.[1]

Earlier philosophers such as Parmenides* and Heraclitus* also influenced Plato. Parmenides described the theory that our sensory faculties prevent us from recognizing the unified, unchangeable, and timeless nature of existence.[2] The theory implied a criticism of Heraclitus, who held that the cosmos existed in a state of perpetual flux.[3] Socrates,* however, was the strongest direct influence on Plato.

For Athenian citizens of Plato's time, "the nature of virtue" was

❝ In both its form and its content ... *The Symposium* is intimately related to Plato's larger ethical concerns with the nature of the good life. Erotic relationships, of the sort that all the speakers are concerned with, and which typically took place at symposia, were an important way in which virtue was transmitted. ❞

Frisbee C. C. Sheffield, *Plato's Symposium: The Ethics of Desire*

well established as a subject for debate, both inside and outside of symposium.[4] The concept of Eros was generally seen as an equivocal*—ambiguous—external force that needed regulating.[5] Eros could be portrayed as making characters act against their will in the tragedies of dramatic theatre, or used to conceptualize the irrational behavior of the citizens' assembly when swayed by the speech of a politician.[6]

Overview of the Field

It is worth considering what Plato thought and wrote about the sophists,* a section of the intellectual class who taught rhetoric* (how to talk and discuss effectively) and the arts of disputation* (arguing and debating) for financial reward. The sophists, of whom Plato asserts in his *Protagoras* that they believed they could teach virtue, were enticing to their audiences. But conservative sections of society disapproved of them. Plato criticized them rigorously throughout his work, saying they were only really interested in money and hedonism* (the pursuit of pleasure) and thus posed a risk to the souls of their impressionable students.

For Plato, philosophy was both a form of education and a practice to be lived. He believed it should be taught for free, and the sophists were incapable of embodying this virtue, one of the discipline's main aims.[7] Plato was greatly troubled by the damaging effects on education of the forms of rhetoric taught by the sophists. His inquiry into the use of Eros in philosophy should be considered against the background of these anxieties.

The influence on Plato's thinking of ancient Greece's literary traditions should also be noted. The epic poems* attributed to Homer* shaped Greek notions of morality generally, while the comic and tragic playwrights active in the Athens of the fifth century b.c.e. influenced Plato's thinking more specifically. Indeed, *Symposium* features characters who were themselves playwrights, and adapts motifs, images, and ideas that had been explored in the theater (notably that of the irresistible power and effects of Eros). In Greek literature, Eros had generally been presented as an irresistible external force that could drive an individual to act against their better judgment or good advice.[8] Plato's more positive depiction of Eros must be considered in this light.

Academic Influences

Aristotle records that Plato's first philosophical experience came from the Heraclitean* philosopher Cratylus, with whom Plato associated as a young man.[9] While Plato incorporated certain of Heraclitus's ideas into his thought, he rejected his central theory that everything was in a state of flux, or more precisely, that the stability of the whole was only achieved through constant alteration. In distinction, Plato's metaphysics would go on to contrast this Heraclitean world of perceptible change with a prior and more perfect world of unchanging forms, whose intellectual apprehension held the key to true knowledge and virtue.[10]

Undoubtedly the most important direct influence on Plato was his teacher Socrates, to whom Plato gives a central role in *Symposium*. However, it is difficult for scholars to distinguish the views of Socrates himself from those of Plato[11] because we have no firsthand record of Socrates' own beliefs. The establishment of clear lines of influence from one to the other is at the root of what is known as the "Socratic Problem," an issue that has been with us so long that it has been described as "insoluble."[12]

Through its response to the debate of the time about the relationship between erotic desire and philosophy, *Symposium* fundamentally altered the shape of that discussion. In the dialogue's longest speech, that of Socrates, Plato reinterprets Eros as an internal force capable of motivating philosophical reflection and the pursuit of virtue.[13] In this way he questions the prevailing view of Eros as an invasive force that provokes irrational behavior.

Plato achieves his purpose by giving an account of a fictional symposium. While this was not an entirely new literary device in itself, his was the first piece of work to portray a symposium in order to conduct a philosophical exploration of ethics and desire. As a result we can say that the book's seminal nature is derived from the combination of its literary form and its philosophical content.

Symposium did not emerge from a vacuum, as an act of pure originality, but drew from the literary, philosohical, and social environment of the period's culture. Plato's innovation lies in his bringing unfamiliar ideas and categories into conversation with one another to create something radically new.

NOTES

1 W. K. C. Guthrie, *A History of Greek Philosophy,* vol. 4, *Plato: The Man and His Dialogues: Earlier Period* (Cambridge: Cambridge University Press, 1986), 35–6.

2 Guthrie, *History of Greek Philosophy,* vol. 4, 34–5.

3 Guthrie, *History of Greek Philosophy,* vol. 4, 33.

4 Frisbee C. C. Sheffield, *Plato's Symposium: The Ethics of Desire* (Oxford: Oxford University Press, 2006), 4–5.

5   Sheffield, *Plato's Symposium*, 5.

6   Richard Hunter, *Plato's Symposium* (Oxford: Oxford University Press, 2004), 16–8.

7   Marina McCoy, *Plato on the Rhetoric of Philosophers and Sophists* (Cambridge: Cambridge University Press, 2011), 1–3.

8   Hunter, *Plato's Symposium*, 17.

9   Debra Nails, *The People of Plato: A Prosopography of Plato and Other Socratics* (Indianapolis: Hackett Publishing, 2002), 105–6.

10 Guthrie, *History of Greek Philosophy,* vol. 4, 33.

11 William Prior, "Socrates (historical)," in *The Continuum Companion to Plato*, ed. Gerald A. Press (London: Continuum, 2012), 29–30.

12 Prior, "Socrates (historical)," 29.

13 Plato, *Symposium*, trans. M. C. Howatson, ed. M. C. Howatson and Frisbee C. C. Sheffield (Cambridge: Cambridge University Press, 2008), 32–50.

MODULE 3
THE PROBLEM

KEY POINTS

- *Symposium* looks to answer two key questions. What is the true nature of Eros?* And what is its relation to the philosophical pursuit of truth and virtue?
- Eros was generally thought of as an intrusive and unknowable external force, often going against reason.
- Plato moves beyond the generally held view by suggesting that erotic desire *can* provide a basis for the pursuit of virtue and wisdom and a true understanding of beauty.

Core Question

The overall core question that Plato's *Symposium* addresses is whether or not Eros has any place in the pursuit of philosophy. Plato finds that it does and suggests it is important for the ethical well-being of the individual and also for the cohesion of the community. To understand the particular importance given to Eros in *Symposium*, it is necessary to consider Plato's specific understanding of the cultural context in which he worked.

The text's inquiry takes place in a fictional symposium—a culturally significant social occasion attended by ancient Athens's men of high status.[1] One important aspect of the ancient symposium was its role as a venue for the practice of pederasty,* an arrangement between men of different ages according to which the junior partner was instructed in virtue and knowledge by the elder in exchange for sexual pleasure.[2]

In these relationships, of course, erotic desire for the body of another was central. Although these arrangements were scrutinized

> **❝** As Eros is [traditionally] an invasive force from outside, its presence can be shaming and disorienting, in that it takes away one's better judgment and one's sense of independence; Eros forces us to confront our lack and need, ideas which are to be fundamental to *Symposium.* **❞**
>
> Richard Hunter, *Plato's Symposium*

and often liable to charges of corruption, *Symposium* explores the ways in which such relationships might demonstrate, develop, or serve as a foundation for different aspects of virtue and wisdom. This is especially true of the long speech that Plato gives to Socrates.*

The Participants

Eros had previously been depicted in Greek literature as an important physical principle that allowed mortal beings to reproduce and also drove the fertility of their natural environment. Eros was said to make itself felt through a desire similar to the desire the rain feels for the ground.[3]

In general, "Eros in archaic poetry may, in the broadest terms, be thought of as an invasive force or emotion which drives one to wish to satisfy a felt need."[4] This "invasive force" was often presented as an ambiguous power that overwhelmed its subject and caused individuals to act irrationally in pursuit of their desire. As this invasion was typically framed as an act of the gods, Eros was also seen as a kind of divine power. In Euripides'* plays *Medea* and *Hippolytus*, for example, the characters of Medea and Phaedra both experience this uncontrollable force.[5] It is associated with an overwhelming feeling of a lack of what they desire and an equally irresistible urge to fill that lack.

It was this conception of Eros that formed the intellectual and cultural background to Plato's own discussion of the subject in

Symposium.
The Contemporary Debate

By considering the possibility that, rather than being an unmanageable external influence, Eros might be both generated internally and might lead to the attainment and maintenance of virtue, Plato goes against the dominant views of his time.

Plato has each speaker compete in giving an *encomium*—that is, a speech of praise—on the subject of Eros. While this blurs the boundary between the serious and the comic, and sees Plato engaging in both artistic parody and abstract philosophical argument, Eros is described throughout in positive terms. By associating erotic desire with lack (especially in the speech given to Aristophanes,* who defines it as "the desire and pursuit of the whole"),[7] Plato highlights an idea that would certainly have been familiar to his peers. Similarly, the idea that Eros is associated with a lack of reason is represented in *Symposium* by the speech Plato gives to Alcibiades,* who describes philosophy as a "madness and frenzy" caused by the venomous bite of Eros to the "heart or soul."[8]

The polyphonic* nature of the text—that is, the inclusion of several voices—and the fact that it is presented as a secondhand (reported) account, makes it difficult to perfectly define its philosophical argument. Nevertheless, the sixth speech, the one given to Socrates, has generally been seen to offer *Symposium*'s central conclusion, given that the ideas it describes overlap with central ideas Plato portrays elsewhere in his body of work.

NOTES

1   Richard Hunter, *Plato's Symposium* (Oxford: Oxford University Press, 2004), 5–7.

2   Hunter, *Plato's Symposium,* 5–7; Frisbee C. C. Sheffield, introduction to *Symposium*, by Plato, trans. M. C. Howatson, eds. M. C. Howatson and Frisbee C. C. Sheffield (Cambridge: Cambridge University Press, 2008), viii–x.

3   Hunter, *Plato's Symposium*, 17.

4   Hunter, *Plato's Symposium*, 16.

5   Hunter, *Plato's Symposium*, 17–8.

6   Plato, *Symposium*, trans. M. C. Howatson, ed. M. C. Howatson and Frisbee
     C. C. Sheffield (Cambridge: Cambridge University Press, 2008), 32–50.

7   Plato, *Symposium*, 26.

8   Plato, *Symposium*, 57.

THE AUTHOR'S CONTRIBUTION

KEY POINTS

- Erotic desire can lead the philosopher to the sight of the very Form of Beauty* itself, from which comes true virtue.

- *Symposium* makes original arguments about Eros's* positive contribution both to the virtuous life and the nature of beauty. In writing it, Plato created a new form of philosophical literature.

- In ancient Greece, symposia provided a place for erotic practices, education, instruction, and ethical debate and conversation. Plato makes use of this connection for his own philosophical ends.

Author's Aims

In *Symposium*, Plato's chief aim is to discuss the relationship between Eros and ethics, happiness, truth, and education. In doing so, Plato moves away from the philosophical inquiries of his contemporaries by conjoining the realms of morality, ethics, and Eros. He does this through an elaborate literary construction in which key ideas are skilfully embedded in a narrative (in this instance, a fictional dialogue taking place at a symposium).

Symposia had previously been used as settings for thinking about ethics by poets of the sixth century b.c.e. such as Theognis of Megara* and Alcaeus of Mytilene.* The historian Herodotus* (fifth century b.c.e.) described them in a celebrated book on the history and peoples of the Mediterranean region.[1] It is Plato's account, however, with its depth of philosophical ideas and its depiction of wise men at intellectual play, that is considered to be the source of viewing the symposium as a learned dinner party where philosophy is served in an

> **❝** The correct way for him to go ... to the things of love, is to begin from the beautiful things of the world, and using these as steps, to climb ever upwards for the sake of that other beauty, going from one to two and from two to all beautiful bodies, and from beautiful bodies to beautiful practices, and beautiful practices to beautiful kinds of knowledge, and from beautiful kinds of knowledge finally to that particular beauty which is knowledge solely of the beautiful itself, so that at last he may know what the beautiful really is. **❞**
>
> Plato, Socrates'* speech in *Symposium*

entertaining fashion.[2]

The themes of the text emerge from the speeches given by each of the seven characters at symposium. Plato's structuring of this fictional event is designed to allow the speeches to enrich and complement, critique and modify, restate and undercut the ideas and themes that arise.

Socrates' speech, the sixth, being the longest and the most philosophically rich, is said to embody the central themes of the work and to resolve the questions raised by the other speeches.[3] Here Plato explores the original idea that erotic desire can provide a positive and fruitful foundation for the philosophical pursuit of wisdom and virtue when that desire is acted upon "correctly."

Approach

Each of the seven speakers in *Symposium* delivers a speech in praise of Eros. While each one is important for an understanding of the text as a whole, the speech Plato gives to Socrates offers the most surprising investigation of Plato's core question. It is notably inventive in its suggestion that the erotic desire for beauty is capable of making a positive contribution to the philosophical pursuit of virtue and wisdom.

This is detailed most famously in the passage concerning the Ascent to Beauty,* according to which the person who has allowed Eros to take hold progresses from the experience of beautiful bodies to the love of beautiful souls, and from there to the appreciation of beauty in laws and institutions and branches of knowledge. The final step is the sight and understanding of the Form of Beauty, something that exists outside the changing world of appearances.[4]

The key point that Plato's Socrates makes in his speech is that when erotic desire for what is beautiful is pursued in the right way and in the right order, it will be beneficial to the acquisition of virtue and wisdom. In this sense, erotic desire is seen as positively related to reason and philosophy, rather than a hindrance.

Although it is intended to be a significant speech, the literary construction of the whole text with its multiple narrators prevents us from forming firm conclusions based on Socrates' words alone. Indeed, after he has finished speaking, the whole dynamic of *Symposium* changes when the boisterous politician Alcibiades* intrudes with a crowd of partygoers and alters the mood with a rather drunken speech in praise of Socrates himself.[5] Plato uses the discourse of Alcibiades to highlight the difficulty of analyzing Socrates and uncovering the truth and wisdom in his words.[6] The speech tells us that "reading this or any work of Plato requires effort and thought, requires us in fact to 'get inside' Socrates' words."[7] Mingling the literary with the philosophical in this way, Plato's approach in *Symposium* is both innovative and appealing for the reader.

Contribution In Context

By considering the possibility that Eros might be an internal force conducive to the flourishing of virtue, Plato resists the commonly held views of his time.

A symposium provided a setting where erotic activities took place alongside education and instruction, particularly in the elite practice of pederasty.*8 For Plato to frame his philosophical exploration as a dialogue taking place at one of these events was innovative.

Despite using a literary form considered out of the ordinary in its day, the work nevertheless draws on the ideas of earlier philosophers. For example, *Symposium*'s inquiry into the role and importance of Eros borrows from Empedocles,* a philosopher of the mid fifth century b.c.e., most notably in the speeches Plato gives to Aristophanes* and Eryximachus.*9 Empedocles presented a vision of the natural evolution and alteration of the universe as being driven by the competing forces of strife and love—although he uses the Greek word *philia* (love or friendship) rather than Plato's more intense Eros (the force of love or desire). Plato's exploration of Eros translates Empedocles' cosmic force into an internal source of power capable of uniting individuals with those they love, while offering the possibility of limitless virtue.

In the speech Plato gives to Socrates, beauty is described as abstract and unchanging. Contemplation of beauty, Socrates tells us, generates true wisdom. This is an idea adapted from Parmenides of Elea,* a philosopher of the early fifth century b.c.e. who believed that the sensible world (that is, the world we can perceive with our senses) was a deceptive version of a true, unchanging, and eternal reality in the form of a perfect sphere. Plato's Theory of Forms* and their role in the attainment of knowledge owes something to this idea. In *Symposium* we read that the practice of philosophy allows us to transcend the material world and attain the realm of abstract beauty. Plato differs from Parmenides in his belief that Eros had a role to play in the education needed to ascend to a glimpse of the ideal Form of Beauty.

NOTES

1 Richard Hunter, *Plato's Symposium* (Oxford: Oxford University Press, 2004), 14–5.

2 Hunter, *Plato's Symposium,* 9–10, 126.

3 Plato, *Symposium*, trans. M. C. Howatson, ed. M. C. Howatson and Frisbee C. C. Sheffield (Cambridge: Cambridge University Press, 2008), 32–50.

4 Plato, *Symposium*, 48–9.

5 Plato, *Symposium*, 51–63.

6 Plato, *Symposium*, 55–7.

7 Hunter, *Plato's Symposium*, 11.

8 Hunter, *Plato's Symposium,* 5–7; Frisbee C. C. Sheffield, introduction to *Symposium*, by Plato, trans. M. C. Howatson, eds. M. C. Howatson and Frisbee C. C. Sheffield (Cambridge: Cambridge University Press, 2008), viii–x.

9 Catherine H. Zuckert, *Plato's Philosophers: The Coherence of the Dialogues* (Chicago: University of Chicago Press, 2009), 289–90.

SECTION 2
IDEAS

MODULE 5
MAIN IDEAS

KEY POINTS

- *Symposium* explores the nature of Eros* and its relation to philosophical and ethical life.

- Erotic desire, pursued in the right manner and sequence, can generate virtue and wisdom.

- The text is a series of speeches at a specific kind of social event. Every speech in praise of Eros qualifies the other.

Key Themes

In Plato's *Symposium* we follow a fictional debate on the nature of erotic love—Eros—and its relation to wisdom and the ethical life.

Asked "to make a speech in praise of Love,"[1] each participant at a symposium presents an alternative definition of Eros, incorporating ideas taken from myth, literature, medicine, history, and philosophy. Through this dialogue, the text discusses key ethical, social and educational themes: how to teach wisdom; how to instil a sense of respect and bravery; how to maintain physical, emotional and spiritual health; how inspiration and excellence emerge; how one might attain wisdom, truth and happiness through the contemplation of beauty.

The central speech, given by Plato to Socrates,* seeks to explain the ways in which erotic desire can provide a foundation for the philosophical pursuit of truth and virtue—assuming that the desire is acted upon correctly.

The form in which these ideas are presented (a series of speeches by men at a social event) also allows *Symposium* to address themes such as the nature of male friendship, and to provide a commentary on the effects of rhetoric* on truth—a concern that runs through much of Plato's work.[2]

❝ Anyone who has been guided to this point in the study of love and has been contemplating beautiful things in the correct way and in the right sequence, will suddenly perceive, as he now approaches the end of his study, a beauty that is marvellous in its nature—the very thing ... for the sake of which all the earlier labors were undertaken. ❞

Plato, Socrates' speech in *Symposium*

Exploring The Ideas

The clearest outline of Plato's key ideas is presented in the words he puts into the mouth of Socrates.

Socrates declares that the speeches that have been made before his have glorified the speaker rather than the nature of Eros.[3] Those speeches, he says, praised the quality of those who are loved, rather than Eros itself as it moves the lover. For Socrates, erotic love is defined as a compulsive striving after what is most beautiful. And what is most beautiful must be that which is most good: "The fact is that the only thing people love is the good."[4]

However, this pursuit does not end with possession of "the good." Its object is to generate "wisdom and the rest of virtue ... the good ordering of cities and households ... moderation and justice."[5] In other words, as a pursuit of what is beautiful and good, Eros is firmly associated with the philosophical life as a practice in its own right. And the aim of this practice is virtue.

Socrates' analysis culminates in a celebrated passage describing the Ascent to Beauty.*[6] In this section, the one who seeks virtue and truth advances from the appreciation of beauty in material things, such as the human body, to the appreciation of things that are not material, such as beautiful souls and forms of knowledge. The final aim is to see and understand the unchanging Form of Beauty* itself. While everything worthy of contemplation has something of beauty in it, the Form of Beauty itself is eternal and unalterable: "It does not come into being or waste away ... It exists on its own, single in substance and everlasting."[7] Erotic desire, if acted upon mindfully (says Socrates), can take us to this level.

Language And Expression

Symposium's main themes emerge from the seven speeches given in the course of the symposium Plato describes. The work is structured to allow the various descriptions of the nature and function of Eros to qualify and enrich one another. As a consequence, we are obliged to consider the text's philosophical ideas and the way those ideas are presented together.

Plato, it seems, was aware of this. He claimed throughout the body of his work that the rhetorical practices of his period were concerned with the persuasion and enchantment of one's audience, rather than with the truth. In what is arguably a self-referential comment, Socrates begins his speech by accusing those who spoke before him of praising themselves rather than Eros, commenting sarcastically that it "seems that the original proposal was not that each should really praise Love but that we should give the appearance of doing so."[8] If rhetoric's purpose is persuasion (as Plato seems to acknowledge), it does not automatically make a "successful" argument true—and it has nothing to do with the purity of the arguer's intentions, either.

It is worth noting that *Symposium's* inquiry into knowledge reaches no definite conclusion. It does not end when Socrates has finished speaking, but when the others present fall asleep.[9]

The text may be difficult to interpret definitively but this is not a shortcoming. It is central to Plato's intention to encourage the reader to continue in the pursuit of wisdom, questioning previous judgements and reassessing the basis of any claim to knowledge. In this sense *Symposium* does not present a closed doctrine for the reader to memorize, but a series of challenges and ideas useful for the practice of philosophy.

Plato's description of the Ascent to Beauty has proved to be one of the most striking images in Western literature and philosophy; indeed, it has been said that it has done "much to mold the European imagination."[10] It brilliantly encapsulates his view of the purpose of philosophical activity and its role in education.

Although the final significance of *Symposium* in the context of Plato's thought as a whole remains open to interpretation, it is true that it transforms the discipline of "philosophy"—that is, the *philia* ("friendly" love) of *sophos* (wisdom)—to an "erotic" (that is, loving and self-perpetuating) desire for wisdom.

NOTES

1   Plato, *Symposium*, trans. M. C. Howatson, ed. M. C. Howatson and Frisbee C. C. Sheffield (Cambridge: Cambridge University Press, 2008), 7.

2   Marina McCoy, *Plato on the Rhetoric of Philosophers and Sophists* (Cambridge: Cambridge University Press, 2011), 1–3.

3   Plato, *Symposium*, 33.

4   Plato, *Symposium*, 43.

5   Plato, *Symposium*, 47.

6   Plato, *Symposium*, 48–9.

7   Plato, *Symposium*, 49.

8   Plato, *Symposium*, 32–3.

9   Plato, *Symposium*, 63.

10 Gregory Vlastos. "The Individual as an Object of Love in Plato," in *Platonic Studies,* ed. Gregory Vlastos (Princeton NJ: Princeton University Press, 1973), 24.

MODULE 6
SECONDARY IDEAS

KEY POINTS

- The speech of Aristophanes* presents an original myth of erotic desire resulting from a primordial lack.

- Aristophanes' speech has been interpreted as conveying an original theory of gender and sexual desire. Its concerns are somewhat different to those of the central speech given to Socrates.*

- The philosophical merit of the speech given to Eryximachus* has often been overlooked.

Other Ideas

The subject of every speech in Plato's *Symposium* is Eros* (the force of desire, often associated with sexual love) and its relation to friendship, ethics and education. Although these reflections reach a culmination in the major discourse of Plato's teacher Socrates, the speeches given to the playwright Aristophanes and the statesman Alcibiades* are also worth noting. Aristophanes and Alcibiades express their ideas by referencing dramatic myth in vivid characterization, and in compelling depictions of both the debilitating and the healing powers of Eros.

The speech given to Aristophanes paints a picture of the origin of the human race through a mythology unique to Plato in which erotic desire has its origin in a very ancient lack.[1] The concluding speech Plato gives to Alcibiades, meanwhile, explores Eros's physical dimensions and its relation to the "madness" of philosophy.

Exploring The Ideas

Aristophanes' mythological depiction of the origin of the human race

> ❝ Each of us is a mere tally of a person, one of two
> sides of a filleted fish, one half of an original whole. We
> are continually searching for our other half. ❞
>
> Plato, the speech of Aristophanes in *Symposium*

is unique to Plato, and one of his most interesting innovations.[2] The speech claims that the current mortal condition of the human race is a degraded state; that we were originally spherical and double (paired one of three ways: male–female, female–female, or male–male) and that Zeus cut us in half as a punishment. Now separated from our other halves, we humans are compelled to search for the part that completes us. It is this original pairing (according to Plato's Aristophanes) that determines the object of our erotic desires.

As a consequence, Eros is portrayed as a healer capable of bringing mortals back to happiness and wholeness and whose role "is to restore our ancient state by trying to make unity out of duality and to heal our human condition."[3] Desire, in other words, has its origin in an ancient lack, and an individual who doesn't resolve this deficiency is consigned to a state of depression and lethargy. This idea is contrary to the Greek consensus on sexual categories and gender.[4]

Being less focused on the relationship between Eros, education and virtue, such a depiction of Eros is distinct from other ideas in *Symposium*. It offers a startling vision of Eros and the challenge of emotional fulfillment that has fascinated subsequent generations of readers.[5]

The speech of Alcibiades, like that of Socrates, discusses the role of Eros in the formation of true virtue and in the philosopher's Ascent to Beauty.* Coming at the end of *Symposium*, the speech pulls the reader back from the abstract intellectualism of Socrates to the physical and emotional desires of individuals.[6] Alcibiades' characterization of philosophy as a "madness and frenzy" caused by the venomous bite of

Eros to the "heart or soul"[7] differs from Socrates' more harmonious account of the erotic Ascent to Beauty, and is more in keeping with the dominant contemporary view of Eros as an invasive, destabilizing force.

After receiving such a bite, Alcibiades says, "there is nothing [a man] will not do or say."[8] Plato's decision to present these ideas by means of the historical person of Alcibiades—a controversial politician and general who was assassinated—leaves questions about the complex connections between philosophy, Eros and political life (an underlying theme of the text).[9] The speech also highlights the challenges of interpretation that *Symposium* presents for its readers. It compares Socrates and his discourses to a statue of the god Silenus* which contains smaller, more beautiful, statues within it. "I don't know if anyone else has seen the statues he has inside, but I saw them once, and they seemed to me divine and golden, so utterly beautiful and wonderful."[10]

This is a both a warning against trusting in surface appearances and an indication that the true marvels of virtue may be concealed. This is an important point to remember in interpreting the words of Socrates' and the other speakers.[11]

Overlooked

According to the traditional interpretation, we should look to the speeches of Alcibiades, Aristophanes, and Socrates for Plato's most important metaphysical* ideas. (Metaphysics is the study of the fundamental structures of reality.) However, the speech given to the doctor Eryximachus has perhaps been overlooked, often being regarded as "much less generally accessible" and "taken to be just a parody of the jargon-ridden 'grand unifying theories' of fifth-century science and medicine."[12]

Eryximachus attempts to explain the unity of the arts and sciences in terms of "good" and "bad" kinds of love, taking various disciplines in turn to explain his point.[13] "I shall start by speaking about medicine, in order to give pride of place to that profession,"[14] he announces in a discourse often regarded as self-serving and weighted towards his own preferences[15] (notably perhaps in his somewhat patronizing use of the philosophy of Heraclitus*).[16] Eryximachus's excessive concern with minor details has led some readers to argue that Plato is more interested in caricaturing an intellectual type than in a precise exploration of ideas. As a result, the speech has been dismissed as having little philosophical merit. Yet the idea that Eryximachus does not take himself as seriously as it seems at first has begun to yield insights into how his speech contributes positively to *Symposium*. There remains room for further research of this issue.[17]

NOTES

1   Plato, *Symposium*, trans. M. C. Howatson, ed. M. C. Howatson and Frisbee C. C. Sheffield (Cambridge: Cambridge University Press, 2008), 22–7.

2   Plato, *Symposium*, 22–7.

3   Plato, *Symposium*, 24.

4   Jeffrey Carnes, "The Myth Which is Not One: Construction of Discourse in Plato's Symposium," in *Rethinking Sexuality: Foucault and Classical Antiquity*, ed. David H. J. Larmour et al. (Princeton, NJ: Princeton University Press, 1998), 105.

5   Richard Hunter, *Plato's Symposium* (Oxford: Oxford University Press, 2004), 68–9.

6   Plato, *Symposium*, 51–63.

7   Plato, *Symposium*, 57.

8   Plato, *Symposium*, 57.

9   Cf. Steven Berg, *Eros and the Intoxications of Enlightenment: On Plato's Symposium* (Albany, NY: State University of New York Press, 2010), x–xii, 131–50.

10 Plato, *Symposium*, 56.

11 Deborah Tarn Steiner, *Images in Mind: Statues in Archaic and Classical*

Greek Literature and Thought (Princeton, NJ: Princeton University Press, 2002), 89.

12 Hunter, *Plato's Symposium,* 54.

13 Plato, *Symposium*, 18–22.

14 Plato, *Symposium*, 18.

15 Kevin Corrigan and Elena Glazov-Corrigan, *Plato's Dialectic at Play: Argument, Structure, and Myth in Symposium* (University Park, PA: The Pennsylvania State University Press, 2004), 63.

16 Plato, *Symposium*, 19; Corrigan and Corrigan, *Plato's Dialectic at Play*, 63–5.

17 Hunter, *Plato's Symposium*, 53–9.

MODULE 7
ACHIEVEMENT

KEY POINTS

- Plato's exploration of love, desire, beauty, and virtue in *Symposium* has had an immense influence on Western thought from antiquity* (the period before the Middle Ages) to the present day.

- The text's originality, both in terms of its literary form and its philosophical argument, has guaranteed its continuing importance.

- Christian* mystical* interpretations of the text have sometimes obscured its emphasis on physical sexual desire.

Assessing The Argument

Engaged in parody but committed to the serious activity of philosophy, *Symposium* has been classified as an example of the "seriocomic"* genre: *spoudaiogeloion* in Greek.[1] As a seriocomic text, and noting its subsequent influence on Western intellectual culture as a whole, there can be no question that Plato executed his aims with great success. Blending poetry, rhetoric* and philosophy in a carefully constructed fictional setting, Plato challenges his audience to draw philosophical insight from an occasion which we might compare to a dinner party.

Symposium's playful literary qualities are one of its central aspects and the text became the model for all following works in the seriocomic genre.[2] Plato's aim was to educate while entertaining. In achieving this purpose, he fundamentally altered the discussion of the ways in which desire and erotic love were related to ethics, the pursuit of wisdom, and virtue.

> ❝ *Symposium* has always been one of Plato's most read, most influential, and most imitated works. No doubt this has much to do with the universal appeal of its subject matter ... but it is also the rich variety of the work, together with its accessibility to readers with little philosophical training, which have given it a place of honour in the reception of Platonic ideas. ❞
>
> Richard Hunter, *Plato's Symposium*

Symposium has been adapted and referenced in so many different contexts over the last few millennia that its cultural legacy is extremely complex. What can safely be said, however, is that Plato is widely perceived as the intellectual father of the entire Western philosophical tradition.[3] Even though *Symposium* is not a text that can be interpreted in a straightforward manner, its seven speeches on Eros* have provided continual inspiration for philosophers, theologians,* and scholars in other fields.

Achievement In Context

It is difficult to reconstruct the original context in which *Symposium* would have been received. More than two thousand years have passed and there is little material evidence to help us. It is probably fair to assume, however, that the text's immediate audience would have been students of Plato's Academy,* the philosophical school he established in Athens. The fact that Plato founded the Academy indicates the richness of the intellectual culture of the Athens of the day. This must surely have contributed greatly to the work's success, providing an environment that was naturally receptive to Plato's philosophical discussions.

The value placed on philosophical discourse (the wider "conversation," so to speak) enabled Plato to flourish as a thinker and teacher. In *Symposium*, he contributed to this discourse by drawing on recent political, philosophical, and literary history in his vivid depiction of famous Athenian figures such as the philosopher Socrates,* the military general Alcibiades,* and the comic playwright Aristophanes.* This would have held significant appeal for his immediate audience.

Plato's students (notably Aristotle*) and others who wrote responses to the text such as Epicurus (a philosopher of the late fourth century B.C.E. and the founder of the Epicurean* school of philosophy) are responsible for securing its legacy. Epicurus believed the world was ruled by chance and that simple pleasures were to be highly valued. Both Epicurus and Aristotle wrote their own symposia in response to Plato's *Symposium*—although no specific details survive.[4]

Later in antiquity other philosophers such as Philo* and Plutarch* composed symposia modeled on Plato's. Both discussed some of the text's moral and ethical stances critically and used the style of the symposium for their own explorations of serious philosophical ideas in light-hearted settings.[5] Aristotle also responded (indirectly) to Plato's theory of Eros and virtue in his *Nicomachean Ethics*.[6]

Students of Plato's Academy, like Plutarch, continued to respond to the text long after Plato's death. Plutarch specifically focused on Plato's characterization of Eros as a daimon* (an intermediary spirit mediating between divine gods and mortal humans) to explore the role of the daimon in bridging the gap between divine and earthly spheres."[7]

In his work *On Isis and Osiris*,[8] Plutarch also drew on *Symposium* to defend a view of Greek and Egyptian cosmology—the science of the origin and development of the universe—that united Eros, in its divine form, with the Egyptian god Horus*—a religious fusion denoted by the term "syncretism."*

Limitations

Although Plato's *Symposium* explores ethical, philosophical, and cultural issues of the Athens of the early fourth century B.C.E., its literary and philosophical qualities have given it a universal appeal. Historically speaking, however, certain of its ideas have received more prominence than others. After all, different ages will have different priorities, biases and concerns.

With this in mind, it is worth noting the ways in which the text was received in the thinking of the Christian* era, especially after the attention given to it by Plotinus,* a philosopher of the third century C.E.,[9] and Augustine of Hippo,* a Christian thinker responsible for one of the most influential adaptations of *Symposium* for a Christian context. The Ascent to Beauty* in Socrates' speech is understood to be the foundation of Augustine of Hippo's theology* of love,[10] describing the progress of the Christian believer, as if on a ladder, ascending towards the love of the divine.

Centuries later, in the 1400s, the religious philosopher Marsilio Ficino* undertook a Christian retelling of *Symposium*, removing its emphasis on the erotic attraction of male bodies.[11] If this suppression of the more physical ideas about sexual desire and love was typical of the Christian mystical view of Plato's *Symposium*, such views have begun to be reclaimed by recent theorists of sexuality and gender.[12] In this we can say that core ideas from the text continue to organize many of the ways Western thought approaches questions concerning love, desire, and ethics.

NOTES

1   Richard Hunter, *Plato's Symposium* (Oxford: Oxford University Press, 2004), 9.

2   Hunter, *Plato's Symposium,* 9–10, 126.

3   A. N. Whitehead, *Process and Reality: An Essay in Cosmology*, Corrected Edition (New York: The Free Press, 1978), 39.

4   Hunter, *Plato's Symposium*, 14–5.

5   Hunter, *Plato's Symposium*, 121–3; 125.

6   Aristotle, *The Nicomachean Ethics*, trans. David Ross (Oxford: Oxford University Press, 1980), 196–201; Richard Kraut, introduction to *The Blackwell Guide to Aristotle's Nicomachean Ethics*, ed. Richard Kraut (Oxford: Blackwell, 2006), 9; A. W. Price, *Love and Friendship in Plato and Aristotle* (Oxford: Oxford University Press, 1989), 85–6.

7   Robert Eisner, *The Road to Daulis: Psychoanalysis, Psychology and Classical Mythology* (Syracuse, NY: Syracuse University Press, 1987), 220, 222–3; Michele A. Luchesi, "Love Theory and Political Practice in Plutarch," in *Eros in Ancient Greece*, ed. Ed Sanders et al. (Oxford: Oxford University Press, 2013), 217–8.

8   Hunter, *Plato's Symposium,* 131–2.

9   Plotinus, "Love," in *The Enneads*, trans. Stephen MacKenna (London: Penguin Classics, 1991), 174–86; Hunter, *Plato's Symposium*, 130–1.

10   Bernard V. Brady, *Christian Love* (Washington D.C.: Georgetown University Press, 2003), 79.

11   Marsilio Ficino, *Commentary on Plato's 'Symposium' on Love*, trans. Sears Jayne (Dallas, TX: Spring Publications, 1985); Hunter, *Plato's Symposium*, 134.

12   See, for example, David Halperin, "Plato and the Erotics of Narrativity," in *Innovations of Antiquity,* ed. Daniel Selden and Ralph Hexter (New York, NY: Routledge, 1992), 95–126; Shannon Bell, "Tomb of the Sacred Prostitute: *Symposium,*" in *Shadow of Spirit: Postmodernism and Religion*, eds. Phillipa Berry and Andrew Wernick (London: Routledge, 1992), 198–210; Jeffrey Carnes, "The Myth Which is Not One: Construction of Discourse in Plato's Symposium," in *Rethinking Sexuality: Foucault and Classical Antiquity*, ed. David H. J. Larmour et al. (Princeton, NJ: Princeton University Press, 1998), 104–21.

MODULE 8
PLACE IN THE AUTHOR'S WORK

KEY POINTS

- Plato offers a comprehensive, if fragmented, philosophical vision across his works, addressing a wide range of topics.

- *Symposium,* usually dated to Plato's middle period, is linked thematically to his *Lysis* and *Phaedrus,* and to his wider ethical concerns.

- The text is one of Plato's most important and influential texts, particularly because of its distinctive literary form.

Positioning

Although the ordering of Plato's works is an imprecise science, *Symposium* is often held to be a product of his middle period, dating to around 380 b.c.e., when Plato was nearly 50 years of age.[1] In many of his earlier works that focused on questions of ethics and the living of a just life, he used the voice of his former teacher Socrates* to expose the assumptions and beliefs of those claiming to have knowledge.

In this period, Plato's thought seems to have extended to subjects such as the construction of an ideal political state (*The Republic*) and the nature of the soul (*Phaedo*). It is often thought that Plato's *Lysis* was composed before *Symposium*, which seems to refine and develop its central themes—love, desire, education and virtue—into a shorter text.[2]

In *Phaedrus*, Plato again investigates Eros,* beauty, and knowledge, adding to it a more detailed account of his Theory of Forms* and the idea that knowledge is a kind of recollection. Generally thought to have been composed after *Symposium*, *Phaedrus* offers a counterpoint to *Symposium's* ideas. It appears to regard the madness of Eros, for

> **❝**[*Symposium's*] discussion of the nature and goals
> of loving relationships takes us to the heart of Plato's
> concern with the good life and how it is achieved. **❞**
> Frisbee C. C. Sheffield, introduction to Plato, *Symposium*

example, as a force capable of provoking the recollection of the "ideal forms" experienced by the soul before birth and as something beneficial to attaining virtue. Socrates describes this madness as "the best of all forms of divine possession."[3]

For the Socrates who appears in Plato's *Phaedrus*, the desired body is more than a rung on a ladder, with loftier and more abstract ideas of love and beauty on the higher rungs.[4] Interpersonal human relationships are seen as valuable in their own right.[5] But it is worth noting that Plato's two central political texts, *The Republic* and the later *Laws*, come to different conclusions about the role of Eros in the stability of the state.[6]

Integration

Plato's body of work is one of the most significant achievements in the history of philosophy. Although it may be somewhat disparate and difficult to unify, being principally made up of dialogues that do not necessarily lend themselves to a single, authoritative interpretation, *Symposium* can only be properly understood as part of this corpus.

The task of interpreting Plato's work as a unified whole has occupied scholars for centuries. The modern debate on this subject is split between "developmentalist"* and "unitarian"* views.[7] According to the developmentalist stance, Plato's philosophy adopts different psychological, epistemological* and ethical positions as it evolves. According to the "unitarian" view, on the other hand, "there is a systematic unity of Platonic doctrine or belief among all the dialogues."[8]

The fact that these opposing views exist points to the difficulty of finding a clear and systematic set of doctrines in Plato's work. *Symposium*, as a work from his middle period, depicts ideas (among which are the Theory of Forms, the ways in which Eros is related to truth and justice, and the ways in which we might categorize and logically infer things) that are explored and debated in his other works. The most dramatically elaborate of all his dialogues,[9] *Symposium*'s unique significance in Plato's body of work lies in its pioneering literary form.

Significance

Plato is frequently regarded as the father of Western philosophy.[10] As one of his major dialogues, *Symposium*'s significance cannot really be questioned. It has proved to be a remarkably influential text from the time of its initial reception (and its frequent imitation) in antiquity* and throughout the Christian* era that followed. Having "shaped the way that the 'golden age' of classical Athens has been imagined,"[11] it continues to inform scholarship today.

It is perhaps ironic that what makes the text stand out from Plato's other writings (notably its highly literary form and its direct discussion of personal desire) are the very qualities that have sometimes undermined an appreciation of its philosophical richness: "Even those scholars who have read *Symposium* together with the *Phaedo* and the *Republic* as hallmarks of Platonism have had difficulties avoiding a highly selective approach to the text."[12]

Recent scholarship has, however, looked to show how the work's central concerns fit into Plato's thought as a whole. This has led to a renewed awareness of the ways in which the text's key elements are "intimately related to standard Platonic preoccupations: with the nature of the good life, with virtue and with how virtue is acquired and transmitted".[13]

NOTES

1   K. Dover, "The Date of Plato's *Symposium,*" *Phronesis* 10 (1965): 2–20.

2   Cf. Catherine Pickstock, "The Problem of Reported Speech: Friendship and Philosophy in Plato's *Lysis* and *Symposium,*" *New Blackfriars* 82 (2001): 525–40.

3   Plato, *Phaedrus*, trans. Walter Hamilton (London: Penguin, 1973), 56.

4   Plato, *Symposium*, 49–50.

5   Plato, *Phaedrus*, 64–5; A. W. Price, *Love and Friendship in Plato and Aristotle* (Oxford: Oxford University Press, 1989), 85–8.

6   Steven Berg, *Eros and the Intoxications of Enlightenment: On Plato's Symposium* (Albany, NY: State University of New York Press, 2010), 153.

7   William Prior, "Developmentalism," in *The Continuum Companion to Plato*, ed. Gerald A. Press (London: Continuum, 2012), 288–9.

8   Prior, "Developmentalism," 288.

9   Frisbee C. C. Sheffield, *Plato's Symposium: The Ethics of Desire* (Oxford: Oxford University Press, 2006), 3.

10 A. N. Whitehead, *Process and Reality: An Essay in Cosmology*, Corrected Edition (New York: The Free Press, 1978), 39.

11 Richard Hunter, *Plato's Symposium* (Oxford: Oxford University Press, 2004), 113.

12 Sheffield, *Plato's Symposium*, 3.

13 Sheffield, *Plato's Symposium*, 3.Uchitelle, "Lonely Bowlers, Unite: Mend the Social Fabric; A Political Scientist Renews His Alarm at the Erosion of Community Ties," *New York Times*, May 6, 2000, http://www.nytimes.com/2000/05/06/arts/lonely-bowlers-unite-mend-social-fabric-political-scientist-renews-his-alarm.html?pagewanted=all&src=pm, accessed June 7, 2013.

SECTION 3
IMPACT

MODULE 9
THE FIRST RESPONSES

KEY POINTS

- The philosopher Xenophon* argues for a more functional conception of Eros* than Plato; Plato's student Aristotle* emphasizes the love of friendship over erotic love.

- Although it is not known how Plato responded to any critics in his lifetime, the account of Eros given in the later *Phaedrus* relates more to human relationships than that given in *Symposium*.

- The cultural context of Athens and the institutional context of Plato's Academy* allow us to assume that the text would have been the subject of vigorous debate during his lifetime.

Criticism

Our knowledge of critical responses to Plato's *Symposium* is limited both by our uncertainty about when it was written and by the fact that we have so few definite references to it from Plato's critics. Nevertheless, we can identify two strands of initial critical response.

The first of these is *Symposium*[1] of the philosopher Xenophon in which the "star" is, again, the philosopher Socrates.* Here, Xenophon has him sharing his wisdom on the subjects of Eros, virtue, and harmonious urban life.

Xenophon's Socrates presents himself as an expert matchmaker. His skill, we learn, is useful for uniting both people and cities. He is the sort of man who can "develop friendships between States and arrange suitable marriages, and would be a very suitable ally for both States and individuals to possess."[2] As in Plato's text, the philosophy is delivered

> ❝ One cannot be a friend to many people in the sense of having friendship of the perfect type with them, just as one cannot be in [erotic] love with many people at once (for [erotic] love is a sort of excess of feeling, and it is in the nature of such only to be felt towards one person). ❞
>
> Aristotle, *The Nicomachean Ethics*

with humor and irony—but Xenophon makes crucial modifications, and therefore implied criticisms, of Plato's ideas.

Although he acknowledges that the spiritual qualities and aspects of Eros transcend the physical, Xenophon chooses to emphasize the pragmatic value of its "lesser" form: *philia* (that is, the force of friendship, or the force of love associated with friendship). He does so by presenting a vision of love more personal, mutual and reciprocal than that proposed by Plato's Socrates—and one supposedly more beneficial to the city, too.

The second strand of initial critical response to Plato's *Symposium* is that of his former student Aristotle whose *Nicomachean Ethics* is an indirect response to Plato's theory of Eros and virtue. Aristotle downplays the significance of Eros to the practice of philosophy and the virtuous life. For him, Eros is a force of instability, "a sort of excess of feeling,"[3] and while he argues that this can cement perfect friendship between two people, it is too intense to be shared among many. Instead, Aristotle emphasizes the less intense, more reciprocal love of *philia*: "the friendship of men who are good and alike in virtue."[4] Whereas Eros is associated with excess, *philia* is more like a "state of character."[5] In choosing *philia* as the glue that binds people and cities together in mutual virtue, Aristotle—like Xenophon—reacts against the more abstract and transcendental notion of Eros set out by Plato's Socrates in *Symposium*.[6]

Responses

The lack of documentary evidence of direct engagement between Plato and his audience makes it difficult to determine his responses to his critics.

Given that Plato's Academy was a place of learning, and that the intellectual culture of Athens was characterized by vigorous debate, we can assume a critical dialogue about Plato's *Symposium* and its treatment of Eros took place—even if we will never know the course it may have taken. However, it is possible to speculate on the nature of this debate by observing the ways in which Plato's treatment of Eros changes in his later work (although we must be careful not to definitively claim that these modifications were provoked by dialogue between the author and his critics).

Plato's *Phaedrus*, widely believed to have been composed after *Symposium*, is the best place to look. While this dialogue also investigates the role of Eros and *philia* in the pursuit of wisdom and virtue, Plato's presentation of Eros is altered from that of *Symposium*. It can still motivate and intellectually inspire the development of true understanding. But, unlike the vision of Socrates' speech in *Symposium*, the Eros of Plato's *Phaedrus* does not exist to usher the lover from the physical body of his beloved towards the sight of transcendental beauty. Now, both the lover and his beloved journey equally toward truth. As Plato explains, the beloved "experiences a counter-love which is the reflection of the love he inspires."[7]

Although this might seem to anticipate Aristotle's emphasis in his *Nicomachean Ethics* that perfect love be reciprocal—shared between two people[8]—Plato differs from Aristotle in his *Phaedrus*. For him, the "madness" of Eros leads to virtue by way of ethical inspiration. Aristotle, however, distrusts the "excess" of erotic love.[9]

Conflict And Consensus

Putnam's detractors made some good points and he acknowledged as much, wondering whether he had overstated his case in the article. Perhaps the trends in community participation had not fallen as much as he had actually thought.[12] In fact, Putnam has since admitted that the claims in his 1995 article were based upon rather slim evidence, and the following year he also realized he had relied on flawed data.[13] In the book, Putnam attempts to silence his critics by using empirical evidence to show sweeping trends of civic disengagement that have not been remedied by community involvement in a non-traditional area. The most valuable tool at his disposal, Putnam notes, was the DDB Needham Life Style Study.

To a large extent, Putnam's revisions in the *Bowling Alone* book appeared to convince skeptics. One critic acknowledged that while many of the claims in Putnam's article had been cast in doubt, "by adding in large, new data-sets and squeezing them dry, Putnam not only salvaged his argument, he gained the high ground."[14]

NOTES

1   Xenophon, *Conversations of Socrates*, trans. Hugh Tredennick and Robin Waterfield (London: Penguin, 1990).

2   Xenophon, *Conversations of Socrates,* 251.

3   Aristotle, *The Nicomachean Ethics*, trans. David Ross (Oxford: Oxford University Press, 1980), 201.

4   Aristotle, *The Nicomachean Ethics*, 196.

5   Aristotle, *The Nicomachean Ethics*, 200.

6   Richard Kraut, introduction to *The Blackwell Guide to Aristotle's Nicomachean Ethics*, 9.

7   Plato, *Phaedrus*, trans. Walter Hamilton (London: Penguin, 1973), 64.

8   A. W. Price, *Love and Friendship in Plato and Aristotle* (Oxford: Oxford University Press, 1989), 85–6; Catherine Pickstock, "The Problem of Reported Speech: Friendship and Philosophy in Plato's *Lysis* and *Symposium*," *New Blackfriars* 82 (2001): 525–40.

9   Plato, *Phaedrus*, 56; Aristotle, *The Nicomachean Ethics*, 201.

10 See, for example, Price, *Love and Friendship in Plato and Aristotle*.

11 Bernard V. Brady, *Christian Love* (Washington D.C.: Georgetown University Press, 2003), 79.

12 Benedict XVI, *Deus Caritas Est*, encyclical letter on Christian love, December 25, 2005, s.11.

13 See, for example, Frisbee C. C. Sheffield, *Plato's Symposium: The Ethics of Desire* (Oxford: Oxford University Press, 2006); Steven Berg, *Eros and the Intoxications of Enlightenment: On Plato's Symposium* (Albany, NY: State University of New York Press, 2010); Gary Alan Scott and William A. Welton, *Erotic Wisdom: Philosophy and Intermediacy in Plato's Symposium* (Albany, NY: State University of New York Press, 2008).

MODULE 10
THE EVOLVING DEBATE

KEY POINTS

- *Symposium* was the inspiration for a new type of philosophical writing.

- The dialogue's huge influence on Western thought and culture can be seen in Western philosophy, theology, literature, and poetry.

- The text recast discussions about love, desire, virtue, gender, and sexuality. It continues to shape these discussions today.

Uses And Problems

The distinctive literary form of Plato's *Symposium* proved to be particularly inspiring to later writers. The idea of the dinner party as a literary context for the discussion of philosophical ideas was striking enough to be imitated for a very long time. Indeed, Plato's work has been described as "the classic founding text of [a] genre."[1]

We can perhaps also thank *Symposium*, with its speeches given by spirited and humorously portrayed characters, for inspiring the tradition of the ancient novel. In the *Satyricon* of Petronius,* a Roman satirist of the first century c.e., we read tales of unrequited love told at a wild dinner party which recall Alcibiades'* speech in Plato's *Symposium*.[2] Similarly, *The Adventures of Leucippe and Clitophon* by Achilles Tatius* and the *Metamorphoses* of Apuleius* (both writers of the second century c.e.) adapt Plato's innovations for a different audience, notably replacing the homosexual model of desire and virtue with its heterosexual equivalent.[3]

The central question of the text—the place of erotic desire in the

> ** Symposium** became the foundational text for all
> literary dinner parties which followed. **
>
> Richard Hunter, *Plato's Symposium*

search for wisdom and virtue—continued to be important to later
Greek schools of philosophy categorized together as "Hellenistic."*
Zeno* and other early Stoic* thinkers emphasized that Eros could be
beneficial to ethics. These thinkers were part of a school of philosophy,
Stoicism, that believed the virtuous life is best lived in accordance with
nature, indifferent to pain and pleasure. The Stoics sought "to improve
on Plato's own conception of Eros in *Symposium* by further uniting it
with education."[4] Christian* thinkers would later develop these
themes.

The origin of Christian interpretations of Plato's *Symposium* may
be traced back to Plotinus,* a "Neoplatonist" philosopher of the third
century c.e. Neoplatonism was a mystical, philosophical, and religious
system deeply influenced by Plato's works. Plotinus laid the ground
for the subsequent Christian tradition of viewing the Ascent to
Beauty* as a pagan counterpart to the ascent of the Christian soul to
heaven.[5]

Plato's ideas about Eros were adapted for a Christian context by
early theologians* such as Origen of Alexandria,* Gregory of Nyssa,*
and Augustine of Hippo,* in the third to fifth centuries c.e. Augustine's
account of love, for example, is strongly influenced by the passages
concerning the Ascent to Beauty, with this image forming a basis for
his theology of love.[6] In the European period known as the
Renaissance (roughly the fourteenth to the sixteenth centuries),
Symposium was translated by the Italian Leonardo Bruni.* His version,
which censored the more bawdy and physical depictions of Eros, had
great influence on the seminal (but rather sanitized) Christian retelling
of the text by the Catholic scholar Marsilio Ficino.*[7]

Schools Of Thought

Plato's ideas have had a formative influence on all Western thought and culture, especially as a result of their passage into Christian theology through the work of figures such as Augustine of Hippo. They began to re-enter wide circulation in their own right from the Renaissance onwards as artists and intellectuals alike took notice of them. Poets of the nineteenth century, such as Percy Bysshe Shelley,* used Plato's discussions of Eros to define Romantic love.[8] Important writers of the twentieth century have similarly engaged directly with Plato's *Symposium*. In his novel *Maurice*, E. M. Forster* used *Symposium* to explore questions of homosexuality, treating Plato as a lens through which to look at the spiritual and the physical conceptions of Eros, as demonstrated by the contrasting characters of Socrates and Alcibiades* respectively.[9]

Philosophers of all kinds have continued to return to Plato into the twentieth and twenty-first centuries. Among them are Continental* writers such as Martin Heidegger,* Jacques Derrida,* and Michel Foucault.*[10] Modern Platonists in the analytic* tradition adopt a logical and scientific approach to philosophical problems. They take their epistemological* orientation (focusing on the nature and scope of knowledge and how it is acquired) from Plato's theory of the Forms of Beauty,* Truth and Goodness. This theory sees these attributes as transcendental features that exist beyond those objects of the world that we can perceive with our sense organs—"sensible" objects.

According to this view (held to various degrees by philosophers such as Gottlob Frege,* Bertrand Russell,* Hilary Putnam,* and most recently Saul Kripke*), sensible objects function as versions of these abstract forms.[11]

Ideas from *Symposium* have also been adapted by theorists of psychoanalysis,* such as Sigmund Freud* and Jacques Lacan,* to express concepts of desire.[12] Film, art, and opera, too, have frequently turned to *Symposium*, whether in the painting of Peter Paul Rubens* that depicts the moment of Alcibiades'* dramatic arrival at Plato's dinner party,[13] or the film *Hedwig and the Angry Inch** (2001), which engages with Aristophanes'* myth of human desire and the longing to be rejoined to one's other half.

In Current Scholarship

In the present day, Plato's *Symposium* continues to have a wide influence on scholarship. Classical philosophers, scholars of Plato,[14] and Christian* theologians continue, unsurprisingly, to discuss and analyze the work.[15] Literary theorists such as Roland Barthes* have also found much to interest them in Plato's text, particularly in the dialogue's open-ended construction and the complex and ambiguous interactions between the speeches.[16]

Contemporary theorists of gender and sexuality, such as David Halperin,* have noted the work's unusual presentation of sex in the speech of Aristophanes.[17] This has led to debate over the extent to which Plato's ancient text can be taken as a model for contemporary norms of gender and sexual preference. Halperin himself has been keen to stress how modern understandings of sexual orientation do not match the more fluid sense of sexuality that characterized ancient Greece. There is little evidence of a distinct gay culture in ancient Greece, for example, and elite males such as those depicted in Plato's *Symposium* found that having sexual relationships with men was not incompatible with being married to a woman for the purpose of having children.[18]

Halperin has also argued that Aristophanes' speech "stops short of deriving a distinction between homo- and heterosexuality from his own myth just when the logic of his analysis would seem to have driven him ineluctably to it. The omission is telling."[19] This is an important and on-going debate.

NOTES

1   Richard Hunter, *Plato's Symposium* (Oxford: Oxford University Press, 2004), 15.

2   Hunter, *Plato's Symposium*, 126.

3   Hunter, *Plato's Symposium*, 122–3, 127–9.

4   Bernard Collette–Ducic, "Making Friends: The Stoic Conception of Love and Its Platonic Background," in *Ancient and Medieval Concepts of Friendship*, eds. Suzanne Stern–Gillet and Gary M. Gurtler SJ (Albany, NY: State University of New York Press, 2014), 108.

5   Plotinus, "Love," in *The Enneads*, trans. Stephen MacKenna (London: Penguin Classics, 1991), 174–86; Hunter, *Plato's Symposium*, 130–1.

6   Bernard V. Brady, *Christian Love* (Washington D.C.: Georgetown University Press, 2003), 79.

7   Marsilio Ficino, *Commentary on Plato's 'Symposium' on Love*, trans. Sears Jayne (Dallas, TX: Spring Publications, 1985); Hunter, *Plato's Symposium*, 134.

8   Hunter, *Plato's Symposium*, 123–4.

9   E. M. Forster, *Maurice* (London: Penguin, 2005). Hunter, *Plato's Symposium*, 115–7.

10 For a summary, see Drew Hyland, *Questioning Platonism: Continental Interpetations of Plato* (Albany, NY: State University of New York Press, 2004).

11 See Mark Balaguer, "Platonism in Metaphysics," in *The Stanford Encyclopedia of Philosophy,* Spring 2014 Edition, ed. Edward N. Zalta, accessed April 1, 2015, <http://plato.stanford.edu/archives/spr2014/entries/platonism/>.

12 Sigmund Freud, *Beyond the Pleasure Principle*, trans. James Strachey (London and New York: W.W. Norton, 1961), 52; Jacques Lacan, *Écrits: The First Complete Edition in English*, trans. Bruce Fink (New York & London: W.W. Norton, 2006), 699–700; Hunter, *Plato's Symposium*, 117–9.

13 Elizabeth McGrath, "'The Drunken Acibiades': Rubens's Picture of Plato's Symposium," *Journal of the Warburg and Courtauld Institutes* 46 (1983): 228–35.

14 See, for example, Hunter, *Plato's Symposium*; Frisbee C. C. Sheffield, *Plato's Symposium: The Ethics of Desire* (Oxford: Oxford University Press, 2006); Steven Berg, *Eros and the Intoxications of Enlightenment: On Plato's Symposium* (Albany, NY: State University of New York Press, 2010).

15 For example: Catherine Pickstock, "The Problem of Reported Speech: Friendship and Philosophy in Plato's *Lysis* and *Symposium,*" *New Blackfriars* 82 (2001): 525–40; Benedict XVI, *Deus Caritas Est*, encyclical letter on Christian love, December 25, 2005, s.11.

16 Hunter, *Plato's Symposium*, 113; Roland Barthes, *A Lover's Discourse: Fragments*, trans. Richard Howard (London: Vintage, 2002). See also, Jeffrey Carnes, "The Myth Which is Not One: Construction of Discourse in Plato's Symposium," in *Rethinking Sexuality: Foucault and Classical Antiquity*, ed. David H. J. Larmour et al. (Princeton, NJ: Princeton University Press, 1998), 104–21.

17 See, for example, David Halperin, "Plato and the Erotics of Narrativity," in *Innovations of Antiquity,* ed. Daniel Selden and Ralph Hexter (New York, NY: Routledge, 1992), 95–126.

18 David Halperin, *One Hundred Years of Homosexuality: and Other Essays on Greek Love* (London: Routledge, 1990), 15–40.

19 Halperin, *One Hundred Years of Homosexuality*, 18–9.

MODULE 11
IMPACT AND INFLUENCE TODAY

KEY POINTS

- *Symposium* is one of the classic texts of Western philosophy.

- Plato's emphasis on erotic desire in his account of love continues to challenge contemporary thinkers.

- Critics argue that Plato's account of love is insufficiently reciprocal* and leaves too little room for simple affection.

Position

Symposium, a text largely responsible for Plato's reputation as one of the fathers of Western philosophy, is a work of great philosophical and literary originality.[1] Given the extent of its influence on Western thought and culture over more than two thousand years, we should not be surprised that scholars continue to turn to it. The history of how the text has been received and what it reveals about the author and the age in which he lived are interesting in different ways.

What is perhaps surprising is the extent to which the work continues to be used creatively by modern scholars working in a variety of disciplines. Psychoanalysts,*[2] poststructuralist* literary critics,[3] and theorists of gender and sexuality[4] have all turned to it in recent decades, sometimes engaging with the more "traditional" fields of philosophy and theology in their research. Research like this, drawing on methods and theories from across disciplines, is known as "interdisciplinary" in approach. As an example of where interdisciplinary engagement might lead, a Christian* theologian has recently drawn on literary analysis to explore the ways in which the complex construction of *Symposium* is intended as a reminder of the

> ❝ The safest general characterization of the European philosophical tradition is that it consists of a series of footnotes to Plato. ❞
>
> A. N. Whitehead, *Process and Reality: An Essay on Cosmology*

"precariousness and partiality of our attainment to truth."[5]

The fact that the text is still relevant today was recently confirmed when it was used in a court case in the American state of Colorado. Academics were called to debate the view of homosexuality offered by *Symposium* as part of a case about constitutional* amendments and the rights of homosexuals in the present day.[6]

Interaction

Symposium continues to provoke debate among philosophers and theologians on whether its account of erotic love leaves room for affection between people (an argument made recently by the classical scholar Gregory Vlastos,* for example)[7] or whether the form of love it endorses is somewhat impersonal.

The roots of the debate are genuinely ancient—Plato and Aristotle differed in their ideas about what constitutes ideal love, with Aristotle favoring *philia* (the more reciprocal love of friendship) and Plato favoring Eros.* But Plato's emphasis on erotic desire in his analysis of love has continued to challenge contemporary thought. The Danish theologian Anders Nygren,* for example, dismisses Platonic love (and indeed the Eros of the ancient Greeks in general) as fundamentally acquisitive—that is, "self-seeking."[8]

Scholars such as Catherine Osborne have defended Plato from the criticisms of the likes of Vlastos and Nygren by arguing that Plato's account of Eros does in fact provide a basis for a richly interpersonal form of love.[9] Catherine Pickstock has argued that an appreciation of this aspect of the work requires an attentiveness to the "unusual 'literary' devices"[10] that Plato uses, which have often been overlooked by critics. She suggests that the critics have employed a reading of the text that is too literal and fails to appreciate the significance of its disjointed, narrative form for its meaning. Prioritizing how the text itself is structured allows us to see that, for Plato, "friendship itself is structured as a set of friendly exchanges."[11]

The Continuing Debate

Critics of Plato's account of erotic love have engaged with his texts directly, and also opposed the traditions of thought that he has influenced. In the first case, engaging directly with *Symposium*, Gregory Vlastos has argued that Plato presents love of persons simply as a means of reaching something higher, specifically the contemplation of the Beautiful in itself (Vlastos derives this from the Ascent to Beauty* section of Socrates'* speech). So people are regarded merely as instruments, as "placeholders of the predicates 'useful' and 'beautiful',", and Plato "relegate[s] love of persons to the lowest level" in his hierarchy.[12] Vlastos then looks at Aristotle's account of ideal love, which, he says, teaches that "to love another person is to wish for that person's good for that person's sake."[13] Vlastos sees Aristotle's account as far superior to that of Plato.

In turn, Anders Nygren has focused his critique on the ancient Greek concept of Eros in general, and on those forms of Christian theology that, building on Plato, have sought to find a central place for Eros in their theologies of love. Nygren regards erotic desire as basically "egocentric," or self-seeking, and sees this as a deeply inadequate form of love.[14] By contrast, in his view true love is one that purifies itself of any self-seeking motivation. He therefore opposes forms of Christian theology that emphasize Eros, and defends an alternative theology that presents self-sacrificial love as the only "truly" Christian love.[15]

NOTES

1 Richard Hunter, *Plato's Symposium* (Oxford: Oxford University Press, 2004), 113.

2 Hunter, *Plato's Symposium*, 117–9.

3 Shannon Bell, "Tomb of the Sacred Prostitute: *Symposium,*" in *Shadow of Spirit: Postmodernism and Religion*, eds. Phillipa Berry and Andrew Wernick (London: Routledge, 1992), 198–210; Paul Allen Miller, "The Classical Roots of Poststructuralism: Lacan, Derrida, and Foucault," *International Journal of the Classical Tradition* 5 (1998): 209–13.

4 David Halperin, "Plato and the Erotics of Narrativity," in *Innovations of Antiquity,* ed. Daniel Selden and Ralph Hexter (New York, NY: Routledge, 1992), 95–126; Jeffrey Carnes, "The Myth Which is Not One: Construction of Discourse in Plato's Symposium," in *Rethinking Sexuality: Foucault and Classical Antiquity*, ed. David H. J. Larmour et al. (Princeton, NJ: Princeton University Press, 1998), 104–21.

5 Catherine Pickstock, "The Problem of Reported Speech: Friendship and Philosophy in Plato's *Lysis* and *Symposium,*" *New Blackfriars* 82 (2001): 535.

6 Hunter, *Plato's Symposium,* 125; Martha Nussbaum, "Platonic Love and Colorado Law: the Relevance of Ancient Greek Norms to Modern Sexual Controversies," *Virginia Law Review* 80 (1994): 1515–651.

7 Gregory Vlastos, "The Individual as an Object of Love in Plato," in *Platonic Studies,* ed. Gregory Vlastos (Princeton NJ: Princeton University Press, 1973), 3–42.

8 Anders Nygren, *Agape and Eros*, trans. Philip Watson (London: SPCK, 1983).

9 Catherine Osborne, *Eros Unveiled: Plato and the God* of *Love* (Oxford: Clarendon Press, 1994), 222–6; see also Pickstock, "The Problem of Reported Speech," 525–40.

10 Pickstock, "The Problem of Reported Speech," 526.

11 Pickstock, "The Problem of Reported Speech," 530.

12 Vlastos, "The Individual as an Object of Love in Plato," 26.

13 Vlastos, "The Individual as an Object of Love in Plato," 3.

14 Nygren, *Agape and Eros*, 210.

15 Nygren, *Agape and Eros*, 559–60, 721.

MODULE 12
WHERE NEXT?

KEY POINTS

- As a foundational text of Western philosophy, *Symposium*'s importance is unlikely to decline.

- The text's emphasis on erotic desire, its complex narrative structure, and its innovative ideas about gender and sexuality continue to excite scholars.

- The text's striking philosophical insights, its original literary qualities, and the manner of its reception in Western civilization mean we must consider it a seminal work.

Potential

Plato's *Symposium* is a seminal text in Western literature and will almost certainly continue to be relevant. Almost 2,500 years after it was written, people still turn to the work to better understand both ancient Greece and its cultural concerns and the manner in which Plato's ideas have shaped theories of love, desire, and ethics. When we study the different ways in which *Symposium* has been used over many centuries to explain the love of God as the model for love between people, for example, we learn as much about European cultural history as we learn about the text itself.

Scholars of Plato, philosophers, and theologians* continue to consult the text to solve the questions it poses about erotic desire and what the ideal of love might be. But *Symposium*'s influence permeates Western culture beyond questions of scholarship. We can see it in cultural assumptions about love and desire, and the relationship of these things to wisdom, virtue, and happiness. We have seen how *Symposium* has shaped poetry and literature, visual art, and film.

> **❝** Plato's *Symposium* holds unique interest for modern readers. Arguably, no other Platonic dialogue combines a topic of so central importance to Plato's thought with so dramatic a depiction of renowned ancient characters.**❞**
>
> Gary Alan Scott and William A. Welton, *Erotic Wisdom: Philosophy and Intermediacy in Plato's Symposium*

Over the last century, furthermore, there have been innovative uses of the text by psychoanalysts* such as Sigmund Freud* and Jacques Lacan,* by poststructuralist* literary theorists such as Roland Barthes,* and by theorists of gender and sexuality such as Michel Foucault* and David Halperin.*

The use of elaborate literary devices to express profound philosophical arguments makes *Symposium* a complex and enigmatic text that continues to inspire in many contexts. A representative symbol of the unique genius of Plato's literary and philosophical project, *Symposium* will be considered an important work for as long as Western civilization continues to turn to its past to understand itself.

Future Directions

A new generation of Plato scholars is re-exploring the meaning of Plato's emphasis on the erotic and shedding new light on its significance for ancient Greece and the world of today.[1] Some have seen the text's unusual literary characteristics as the key to its interpretation.[2] In addition, some of the most creative responses to the text have come from theorists of literature, gender, and sexuality. The French cultural theorist Michel Foucault's celebrated three-volume *History of Sexuality*, for example, published in the early 1980s, prompted a number of scholars to return to the subject of antiquity,* and in particular to Plato's *Symposium*, which Foucault discusses in volume two.[3] Their aim was to clarify, dispute, and engage with

Foucault's theoretical framework and findings.

The theories of desire proposed in the speech that Plato gives to the playwright Aristophanes,* (the myth that human beings have been split in half and are now driven by desire for reunion) have become a focal point in this debate.[4] Plato's imagining of our sexual orientation as dependent on the composition of our prior whole (either male-female, male-male, or female-female) has been of interest to modern theorists of sexuality such as David Halperin, the American author of *One Hundred Years of Homosexuality*, a collection of essays discussing Greek sexuality.[5]

Aristophanes' myth of split souls is relevant to more recent arguments relating to sexual and gender identity and the extent to which our sexuality is formed by culture and questions of biological determinism* and social construction.* Biological determinism is the theory that individual human characteristics are genetically determined. Social construction is the theory that human values and preferences, including sexual orientation, are determined by the social and cultural context we live in. It has been argued that *Symposium* is far more radical than people might have realized. Perhaps it recasts "sex into a form of philosophy" so that "with Plato and for Plato, we remake sex."[6]

Likewise, feminist thinkers have looked to Plato's *Symposium* to find a stronger acknowledgement of female sexuality. It has been suggested that Plato offers glimpses of a more inclusive vision of femininity and the possibilities of feminine knowledge according to which women are not defined by a disempowering "lack" decided by culture on their behalf.[7] According to this view, Plato paves the way toward a theory of sexuality that might help us resist the models of sex and gender that arose after him.

Summary

Plato's *Symposium* gave rise to a new type of philosophical literature: the seriocomic* dinner party where weighty philosophical ideas are discussed in a lighthearted manner. It has attracted many imitators, both ancient and modern.[8] Within its dynamic and lively portrait of memorable historical figures such as Socrates,* Aristophanes, and Alcibiades,* there exist passages of philosophical speculation, myths of human sexuality, and examinations of the relationship between the passion of Eros* and ethics. These subjects have fascinated readers and critics for thousands of years.

Symposium is a text that contains some of Plato's finest literary writing, combining metaphor and parody, lucid reasoning, and rhetorical* showmanship. Philosophical ideas that occur elsewhere in Plato's work, such as the theory of Intelligible Forms* that exist outside of the world we can perceive with our senses, are deployed here with a remarkable lyricism. The speech that Plato gives to Socrates on the spiritual journey from bodily erotic desire to the sight of the abstract Form of Beauty* has had an enormous influence on much of Western thought and culture, notably Christian.

The significance of *Symposium* extends beyond Plato's ideas and the form in which he chose to express them. The work's reception over time and the depth of its cultural influence on Western civilization as a whole mean it continues to be one of the greatest-ever works in the arts and humanities.

NOTES

1   See, for example, Frisbee C. C. Sheffield, *Plato's Symposium: The Ethics of Desire* (Oxford: Oxford University Press, 2006); Steven Berg, *Eros and the Intoxications of Enlightenment: On Plato's Symposium* (Albany, NY: State University of New York Press, 2010); Gary Alan Scott and William A. Welton, *Erotic Wisdom: Philosophy and Intermediacy in Plato's Symposium* (Albany, NY: State University of New York Press, 2008).

2   See, for example, Catherine Pickstock, "The Problem of Reported Speech: Friendship and Philosophy in Plato's *Lysis* and *Symposium,*" *New Blackfriars* 82 (2001): 125–40.

3   Michel Foucault, *The Use of Pleasure*, vol. 2 of *The History of Sexuality,* trans. Robert Hurley (New York: Random House, 1990), 230–3, 235–42.

4   Plato, *Symposium*, trans. M. C. Howatson, ed. M. C. Howatson and Frisbee C. C. Sheffield (Cambridge: Cambridge University Press, 2008), 22–7.

5   David Halperin, *One Hundred Years of Homosexuality: and Other Essays on Greek Love* (London: Routledge, 1990), 15–40; Jeffrey Carnes, "The Myth Which is Not One: Construction of Discourse in Plato's Symposium," in *Rethinking Sexuality: Foucault and Classical Antiquity*, ed. David H. J. Larmour et al. (Princeton, NJ: Princeton University Press, 1998), 104–21.

6   Carnes, "The Myth Which is Not One", 120.

7   Shannon Bell, "Tomb of the Sacred Prostitute: *Symposium,*" in *Shadow of Spirit: Postmodernism and Religion*, eds. Phillipa Berry and Andrew Wernick (London: Routledge, 1992), 198–210; Anne-Marie Bowery, "Diotima Tells Socrates a Story: A Narrative Analysis of Plato's *Symposium,*" in *Feminism and Ancient Philosophy*, ed. Julie K. Ward (London: Routledge, 1996), 175–94.

8   Richard Hunter, *Plato's Symposium* (Oxford: Oxford University Press, 2004), 9–10.

GLOSSARY

GLOSSARY OF TERMS

Academy: an influential philosophical school founded by Plato in about 387 B.C.E. in a place just outside Athens, sacred because it was the burial ground of the ancient hero Academus. It flourished until about 87 B.C.E.

Analytic philosophy: a branch of contemporary philosophy considered dominant in Anglo-American philosophical research, and often contrasted in style and method with "Continental philosophy." It adopts a logical and scientific approach to philosophical problems, insisting on the need for the verification of information through the use of rigorous proofs borrowed from mathematics and logic.

Antiquity: the period of ancient history, particularly referring in common usage to the "classical" civilizations prior to the Middle Ages, especially those of Greece and Rome.

Ascent to Beauty: according to Plato, Eros can give us the desire to climb, as if on a ladder, from the sight of a beautiful body to the sight of the eternal Form of Beauty itself. The first "rung" of the ladder in the Ascent to Beauty is the love of a beautiful body. The intermediate stages are an appreciation of all beautiful bodies, the love of beautiful souls, the love of the beauty of institutions and laws, and the love of the beauty of knowledge; the final rung is the sight of the Form of Beauty itself and the true virtue this sight affords.

Biological determinism: the theory that individual human characteristics, including sexual and other preferences, are genetically determined.

Christian: relating to Christianity, a global religion based on the teachings of Jesus Christ and the Bible. It is one of the three great "monotheistic" (belief in one God) religious systems, along with Judaism and Islam.

Civic identity: those things that define the position and obligations of a person who lives in an urban place (in this case, the city-state of ancient Athens).

Constitutional: concerning a set of established principles for the governing of a nation or state (such as the US constitution).

Continental philosophy: the branch of contemporary philosophy dominant in Continental Europe throughout the twentieth century, and usually distinguished in style and methodology from the "analytic philosophy" dominant in Anglo-American philosophy.

Daimon: in ancient Greek thought and belief, a daimon was an intermediary supernatural being who often communicated between the gods and humanity.

Developmentalist: the scholarly view that Plato's philosophy developed throughout his work as he modified his philosophical and psychological positions.

Disputation: the skill and techniques required to win a public debate through persuasion.

Eleusinian Mysteries: secret religious rites that took place at Eleusis in ancient Greece for initiation into the cult of the goddesses Demeter and Persephone.

Epic poems: long poems, which typically in ancient literature, narrated in poetic form a story or legend related to some heroic figure.

Epicureanism: an ancient school of philosophy founded in Athens by the philosopher Epicurus that viewed the world as ruled by chance and saw simple forms of pleasure as the highest good.

Epistemology: the subdiscipline of philosophy concerned with the nature and scope of knowledge, and the methods by which knowledge may be acquired.

Equivocal: open to interpretation; ambiguous. Eros was considered an "equivocal" force since it was difficult to say for certain whether its effects were positive or negative.

Eros: the ancient Greek word for the form of love associated with sexual desire, from which the modern term "erotic" is derived.

Ethnography: the scientific description of peoples and cultures, with their customs, habits, and points of difference.

Form of Beauty: the unchanging and eternal "essence" of beauty, described by Plato as a "wondrous vision"; the sight of the Form of Beauty affords true virtue.

Hedonism: the doctrine or theory of ethics in which pleasure is regarded as the chief good, or the proper end of action.

Hedwig and the Angry Inch: an award-winning American film of 2001 directed and adapted from his own stage play by John Cameron Mitchell. The film makes frequent references to Aristophanes' speech in *The Symposium*.

Hellenistic philosophy: the various schools of thought that arose in Hellenistic (ancient Greek) civilization after Aristotle, including Stoicism, Epicureanism, and ending with Neo-Platonism.

Horus: a god who, in ancient Egyptian mythology, protected the monarchy, frequently depicted as a man with the head of a falcon.

Intelligible Forms: ideas that can be perceived by the intellect and which structure human understanding.

Metaphysics: a subdiscipline of philosophy studying the fundamental structures of reality.

Mystical: concerning religious mysticism, that is, spiritual forms of religious belief, practice or experience that are said to exceed ordinary human understanding.

Neoplatonism: a religious and philosophical school of the third century C.E. derived from a mixture of the philosophy of Plato and various mystical traditions.

Pederasty: an arrangement between men of different ages according to which the junior partner was instructed in virtue and knowledge by the elder in exchange for sexual pleasure

Peloponnesian War: a war between the city-states of Sparta and Athens and their respective empires between 431 B.C.E. and 404 B.C.E., ending in victory for the Spartans.

Polyphony: a term used to describe the effect of the "many voices" that speak in *The Symposium*.

Polytheism: worshipping or believing in more than one god.

Poststructuralism: a body of philosophical and critical work of the twentieth century. Poststructuralists disagree with the theoretical position held by "structuralism" that a text's meaning is found in definite narrative, interpretative, and linguistic structures.

Psychoanalysis: a theory of mind, developed by Sigmund Freud, defined by a method of treatment that attempts to access and interpret the unconscious.

Pythagoreanism: a system of philosophical and religious thought and practice deriving from the teachings of the Greek philosopher and mathematician Pythagoras (570–c.495 B.C.E.), based on the idea that reality is fundamentally mathematical in nature.

Reciprocal: done in return, or concerning exchange.

Rhetoric: the art of discourse, or of persuasive speaking and writing. As a discipline for instructing students in the effective use of language, it has held a central place in the European intellectual tradition from the classical world to the present day.

Roman Catholic Church: the largest Christian Church and one of the oldest religious institutions in the world, led by the Pope.

Seriocomic: a type of literature that combines both serious and comic elements.

Silenus: a minor rural god in ancient Greek religion associated with the major god Dionysus and the activities of dancing and making wine.

Social construction: the theory that human values and preferences, including sexual orientation, are determined by the social and cultural context in which someone lives.

Sophists: paid teachers of philosophy and rhetoric in ancient Greece; often associated with moral relativism, skepticism, and superficial and disingenuous forms of reasoning.

Sparta: a Greek city-state in in the fifth century B.C.E. It defeated Athens in the Peloponnesian War to become the most important city in Greece.

Stoicism: an ancient Greek school of philosophy founded in Athens by Zeno of Citium, which taught that the virtuous life is lived in accordance with nature, and is indifferent to the transience of pain, pleasure and fortune.

Syncretism: the joining together or attempted joining together of different systems of belief into a new whole.

Theologian: a scholar engaged in the study of the nature and works of God.

Theory of Forms: according to Plato's Theory of Forms, everything we are able to perceive with our sense organs is an image or impression of its non-material "Form"—its unchanging, essential counterpart in the "world of Forms." Plato understands the Forms to be the highest and most fundamental kind of reality, but practically impossible to grasp without the most highly refined knowledge.

Treatise: a written text systematically investigating a particular subject (such as a treatise on theology or philosophy).

Unitarian: the scholarly view that Plato's philosophical doctrine and belief are consistent across all his works.

PEOPLE MENTIONED IN THE TEXT

Achilles Tatius was a Greek writer of the second century c.e. Little is known about him apart from his novel *Leucippe and Clitophon*, which imitated stylistic aspects of Plato's *Symposium*.

Agathon (448–400 b.c.e.) was a renowned Greek playwright of tragedies, and a character in Plato's *Symposium*. Although none of his plays survives, we know that in 416 b.c.e., when *Symposium* is set, Agathon would have been celebrating his success at the Lenaia festival in Athens.

Alcaeus of Mytilene was a Greek lyric poet of the sixth century b.c.e. from the island of Lesbos. Although his poetry covers a variety of subjects, he is most noted for the surviving fragments that concern politics and hymns to the gods.

Al Farabi (870-950 c.e) was an Islamic philosopher from Turkestan who studied in Baghdad and travelled widely around the Islamic world. His major philosophical treatise *al-Madina al fadila (The Virtuous City)* is a thorough and detailed engagement with many ideas in Plato's *Republic*. His work exerted considerable influence upon later Islamic philosophers.

Alcibiades (450–404 b.c.e.) was a notorious Athenian general, orator and politician, and a character in Plato's *Symposium*. Known as a brilliant military strategist with a flamboyant personality, he was forced to flee Athens not long after the setting of *Symposium,* and advised her great enemies Sparta and Persia before being assassinated.

Apuleius (125–80 c.e.) was a Latin-language writer and orator who had studied Platonic philosophy. He is known for his risqué satirical novel the *Metamorphosis*, also known as *The Golden Ass*.

Aristophanes (circa 446–386 b.c.e.) was an Athenian comic playwright who features in Plato's *Symposium*. Of his 40 known plays, 11 survive, including *The Clouds*, a play about philosophy and sophistry that portrayed Socrates in a negative light.

Aristotle (384–322 b.c.e.) was an ancient Greek philosopher and student of Plato. He wrote many treatises, the most famous of which are his *Nicomachean Ethics* and his *Metaphysics*. His philosophical work builds, adapts, and expands on the legacy of Plato.

Augustine of Hippo (354–430 c.e.), also known as St. Augustine, was a highly influential early Christian theologian, philosopher, and bishop of the Church. His theology, represented in key works such as *Confessions* and *The City of God,* drew on and adapted Platonic and Neoplatonic ideas.

Roland Barthes (1915–80) was an important French literary theorist and philosopher, who explored ideas around structuralism, poststructuralism and semiotics (the analysis of signs). His works include *Mythologies* and *A Lover's Discourse*, the latter of which draws heavily on Plato's *Symposium.*

Benedict XVI (b. 1927, as Joseph Ratzinger) is a German Roman Catholic theologian and priest. He was Pope of the Roman Catholic Church from 2005 until 2013.

Leonardo Bruni (1369–1444) was an Italian humanist and historian who worked in Florence. He was a notable historian of both antiquity

and his own period, and produced a new translation of Plato's
Symposium.

Jacques Derrida (1930–2004) was a highly influential French
Continental philosopher who developed a form of semiotic analysis
(the analysis of signs) known as "deconstruction." His most famous
works include *Of Grammatology* and *Writing and Difference*.

Empedocles (490–430 b.c.e.) was a philosopher from Acragas in
Sicily. Sections from two of his major works—the *Purifications* and *On
Nature*—survive.

**Eryximachus (circa. 448–late fifth or early fourth century
b.c.e.)** was an Athenian doctor who features as a character in Plato's
Symposium.

Euripides (480–406 b.c.e.) was an ancient Greek playwright. He is
reputed to have written over 90 plays, mainly tragedies, and was one of
the most important figures in the cultural world of classical Athens.

Marsilio Ficino (1433–99) was a key figure in the early Italian
Renaissance. He both translated all the known works of Plato into
Latin and wrote commentaries on them. He famously retold
Symposium in his *De Amore*, "On Love," in a way that sought to
combine Platonic and Christian ideas.

E. M. Forster (1879–1970) was an English novelist. He is known
primarily for his novels *A Room with a View, Howards End* and *A Passage
to India*.

Michel Foucault (1926–84) was a French philosophical and cultural
historian. His work, focusing on theories of power and knowledge,

included a notable study of the history of sexuality in which he engaged with Plato's *Symposium*.

Gottlob Frege (1848–1925) was a German philosopher renowned for his contribution to analytic philosophy in the fields of logic and language. He is famous for works such as *The Foundations of Arithmetic*.

Sigmund Freud (1856–1939) was an Austrian neurologist who is acknowledged as the father of psychoanalysis. Of his many books, among the most famous are *Totem and Taboo, Beyond the Pleasure Principle* and *Civilization and its Discontents*.

Gregory of Nyssa (335–94 c.e.) was an influential theologian and bishop of the early Christian Church from Cappadocia. He incorporated Platonic and Neo-Platonic ideas into his theology in works such as the *Life of Moses*.

David Halperin (b. 1952) is an American theorist of gender and sexuality and, at the time of writing, W. H. Auden Distinguished University Professor of the History and Theory of Sexuality at the University of Michigan. He has worked extensively on ancient and modern theories of sexuality and gender, focusing especially on Plato's erotic theory.

Martin Heidegger (1889–1976) was a German philosopher who has had a significant influence on contemporary philosophy. He is best known for his early work *Being and Time*.

Heraclitus of Ephesus (circa 535–475 b.c.e.) was a philosopher notable for his theory that all things are in a state of flux. Although none of his works survive, we know that he was the author of *On Nature*—a generic title used by many of the early philosophers covering cosmology, physics, morality, and epistemology.

Herodotus (484–425 b.c.e.) was a Greek historian from Halicarnassus renowned for his systematic approach to the subject of history. His major work, the *Histories*, details the war between Greece and Persia.

Homer (circa eighth century b.c.e.) was an ancient composer of epic poetry, of great importance to the ancient Greeks. He is best known as the author of *The Iliad* and *The Odyssey*, which have had a lasting effect on Western thought and culture.

Saul Kripke (b. 1940) is an American philosopher and, at the time of writing, Professor Emeritus at Princeton University. His work focuses on areas including mathematical logic, epistemology, and the philosophy of language. He is the author of *Naming and Necessity*.

Jacques Lacan (1901–81) was a French psychoanalyst who built upon the insights of Sigmund Freud. Lacan's work was published as a series of seminars; the collection Écrits also contains some key essays.

Anders Nygren (1890–1978) was a Swedish theologian of the Lutheran (Protestant) tradition. His most famous work, *Agape and Eros*, argues that Christian love is fundamentally different from Greek Eros.

Origen of Alexandria (circa 185–253 c.e.) was an influential early Christian theologian and philosopher. He made use of Platonic and Neoplatonic ideas in his thinking about God, in numerous sermons, commentaries, and works such as *On Prayer* and *On First Principles.*

Parmenides of Elea (late sixth or early fifth century b.c.e.) was a philosopher. His *On Nature* is a metaphysical work about the division between an intelligible and true world of being, and the sensible and false world of becoming.

Petronius (27–66 c.e.) was a writer and courtier who lived during the Roman Empire. His *Satyricon* contains elements that parody the luxurious lifestyle enjoyed by the emperor Nero.

Philo of Alexandria (20 b.c.e.–50 C.E c.e.) was a Jewish philosopher living in Egypt. His philosophy, notably in his key work *On the Contemplative Life*, attempted to create a synthesis between the ideas of Greek and Jewish philosophy.

Plotinus (204–70 c.e.) was a Greek Neoplatonist philosopher. His idea of the three principles of the One, the Intellect and the Soul, as explored in *The Enneads*, had a strong influence on Christian and Renaissance thought.

Plutarch (46–120 c.e.) was a Greek historian, essayist and biographer from Boeotia. His work *The Amatorius* is influenced by Plato's *Symposium* and likewise takes Eros as its subject

Hilary Putnam (b. 1926) is an American philosopher in the analytic tradition. The author of works such as *Philosophy of Logic*, he specializes in mathematics, computer science, and the philosophy of mind.

Peter Paul Rubens (1577–1640) was a Flemish painter who lived in Antwerp, whose works are typical of the baroque style. He once painted a scene from Plato's *Symposium*.

Bertrand Russell (1872–1970) was a British analytic philosopher, noted for his activities as a mathematician, historian, and social critic. His most famous work is *Principia Mathematica*, which attempted to systematise mathematical study along the lines of logic.

Percy Bysshe Shelley (1792–1822) was an influential English Romantic poet. His work includes the classic poems *Ozymandias*, *Alastor* and *Prometheus Unbound*. He also translated Plato's *Symposium*.

Socrates (469–399 b.c.e.), Plato's primary teacher, was an Athenian philosopher who features in *Symposium* and other of Plato's dialogues. He left behind no writings of his own. He was sentenced to death on charges of corrupting the youth of Athens and impiety.

Solon (638–558 b.c.e.) was a poet, lawmaker and politician in Athens. He introduced legislation designed to address the moral and political problems of the Athenian city-state in the late sixth century, and was revered as one of the seven sages of the ancient world.

Theognis of Megara (circa sixth century b.c.e.) was an ancient Greek lyric poet. All his surviving poetry is set at aristocratic symposia and conveys a wide range of practical, political, and moral advice.

Gregory Vlastos (1907–91) was a scholar of Plato and ancient philosophy. In his *The Philosophy of Socrates*, Vlastos defends the notion that a distinctively Socratic philosophy can be distinguished from that of Plato himself.

Xenophon of Athens (430–354 b.c.e.) was a philosopher and historian of the Greek and Persian empires. He wrote about Socrates and investigated questions of morality, political life, and household management.

Zeno of Citium (334–262 b.c.e.) was an ancient Greek philosopher who established the Stoic school of philosophy in Athens.

WORKS CITED

WORKS CITED

Aristotle. *The Nicomachean Ethics.* Translated by David Ross. Oxford: Oxford University Press, 1980.

Balaguer, Mark. "Platonism in Metaphysics." *Stanford Encyclopedia of Philosophy* Spring 2014 edition, edited by Edward N. Zalta. Accessed April 1, 2015, http://plato.stanford.edu/archives/spr2014/entries/platonism.

Barthes, Roland. *A Lover's Discourse: Fragments*. Translated by Richard Howard. London: Vintage, 2002.

Bell, Shannon. "Tomb of the Sacred Prostitute: *The Symposium.*" In *Shadow of Spirit: Postmodernism and Religion,* edited by Phillipa Berry and Andrew Wernick, 198–210. London: Routledge, 1992.

Benedict XVI. *Deus Caritas Est.* Encyclical letter on Christian love. December 25, 2005.

Berg, Steven. *Eros and the Intoxications of Enlightenment: On Plato's Symposium*. Albany, NY: State University of New York Press, 2010.

Bowery, Anne-Marie. "Diotima Tells Socrates a Story: A Narrative Analysis of Plato's *Symposium.*" In *Feminism and Ancient Philosophy*, edited by Julie K. Ward, 175–94. London: Routledge, 1996.

Brady, Bernard V. *Christian Love.* Washington DC: Georgetown University Press, 2003.

Carnes, Jeffrey. "The Myth Which is Not One: Construction of Discourse in Plato's Symposium." In *Rethinking Sexuality: Foucault and Classical Antiquity*, edited by David H. J. Larmour, Paul Allen Miller, and Charles Platter, 104–21. Princeton, NJ: Princeton University Press, 1998.

Collette-Ducic, Bernard. "Making Friends: The Stoic Conception of Love and Its Platonic Background." In *Ancient and Medieval Concepts of Friendship*, edited by Suzanne Stern-Gillet and Gary M. Gurtler SJ, 87–116. Albany, NY: State University of New York Press, 2014.

Corrigan, Kevin and Elena Glazov-Corrigan. *Plato's Dialectic at Play: Argument, Structure, and Myth in the Symposium*. University Park, PA: Pennsylvania State University Press, 2004.

Dover, K. "The Date of Plato's *Symposium.*" *Phronesis* 10 (1965): 2–20.

Eisner, Robert. *The Road to Daulis: Psychoanalysis, Psychology and Classical Mythology.* Syracuse, NY: Syracuse University Press, 1987.

Ficino, Marsilio. *Commentary on Plato's 'Symposium' on Love.* Translated by

Sears Jayne. Dallas, TX: Spring Publications, 1985.

Forster, E. M. *Maurice: A Novel*. London: Penguin, 2005.

Foucault, Michel. *The Use of Pleasure*. Vol. 2 of *The History of Sexuality*. Translated by Robert Hurley. New York: Random House, 1990.

Freud, Sigmund. *Beyond the Pleasure Principle.* Translated by James Strachey. London and New York: W.W. Norton, 1961.

Guthrie, W. K. C. *A History of Greek Philosophy*. Vol. 4, *Plato: The Man and His Dialogues: Earlier Period.* Cambridge: Cambridge University Press, 1986.

Hadot, Pierre. *Philosophy as a Way of Life: Spiritual Exercises From Socrates to Foucault.* Translated by Michael Chase. Oxford: Wiley-Blackwell, 1995.

Halperin, David. *One Hundred Years of Homosexuality: and Other Essays on Greek Love.* London: Routledge, 1990.

"Plato and the Erotics of Narrativity." In *Innovations of Antiquity,* edited by Daniel Selden and Ralph Hexter, 95–126. New York, NY: Routledge, 1992.

Hunter, Richard. *Plato's Symposium.* Oxford: Oxford University Press, 2004.

Hyland, Drew. *Questioning Platonism: Continental Interpretations of Plato*. Albany, NY: State University of New York Press, 2004.

Kraut, Richard. Introduction to *The Blackwell Guide to Aristotle's Nicomachean Ethics*, edited by Richard Kraut. Oxford: Blackwell, 2006.

Kraye, Jill. "The Transformation of Platonic Love in the Italian Renaissance." In *Plato and the English Imagination,* edited by Anna Baldwin and Sarah Hutton, 76–85. Cambridge: Cambridge University Press, 1994.

Lacan, Jacques. *Écrits: The First Complete Edition in English*. Translated by Bruce Fink. New York and London: W.W. Norton, 2006.

Lear, Andrew. "Ancient Pederasty: An Introduction." In *A Companion to Greek and Roman Sexualities*, edited by Thomas K. Hubbard, 102–27. Chichester: Blackwell, 2014.

Luchesi, Michele A. "Love Theory and Political Practice in Plutarch." In *Eros in Ancient Greece*, edited by Ed Sanders, Chiara Thumiger, Chris Carey and Nick J. Lowe, 209–28. Oxford: Oxford University Press, 2013.

McCoy, Marina. *Plato on the Rhetoric of Philosophers and Sophists.* Cambridge: Cambridge University Press, 2011.

McGrath, Elizabeth. "'The Drunken Acibiades': Rubens's Picture of Plato's Symposium." *Journal of the Warburg and Courtauld Institutes* 46 (1983): 228–35.

Miller, Paul Allen. "The Classical Roots of Poststructuralism: Lacan, Derrida, and Foucault." *International Journal of the Classical Tradition* 5 (1998): 204–25.

Nails, Debra. *The People of Plato: A Prosopography of Plato and other Socratics.* Indianapolis: Hackett Publishing, 2002.

Nussbaum, Martha. "Platonic Love and Colorado Law: the Relevance of Ancient Greek Norms to Modern Sexual Controversies." *Virginia Law Review* 80 (1994): 1515–651.

Nygren, Anders. *Agape and Eros*. Translated by Philip Watson. London: SPCK, 1983.

Osborne, Catherine. *Eros Unveiled: Plato and the God of Love.* Oxford: Oxford University Press, 2002.

Philo of Alexandria. *The Contemplative Life, Giants and Selections.* Translated by David Winston. Mahwah, NJ: Paulist Press, 1981.

Pickstock, Catherine. "The Problem of Reported Speech: Friendship and Philosophy in Plato's *Lysis* and *Symposium.*" *New Blackfriars* 82 (2001): 525–40.

Plato. *Phaedrus.* Translated by Walter Hamilton. London: Penguin, 1973.

—— *The Symposium*. Translated by M. C. Howatson. Edited by M. C. Howatson and Frisbee C. C. Sheffield. Cambridge: Cambridge University Press, 2008.

Plotinus. "Love." In *The Enneads*, translated by Stephen MacKenna, 174–86. London: Penguin Classics, 1991.

Price, A. W. *Love and Friendship in Plato and Aristotle.* Oxford: Oxford University Press, 1989.

Prior, William. "Developmentalism." In *The Continuum Companion to Plato*, edited by Gerald A. Press, 288–9. London: Continuum, 2012.

"Socrates (historical)." In *The Continuum Companion to Plato*, edited by Gerald A. Press, 28–30. London: Continuum, 2012.

Scott, Gary Alan and William A. Welton. *Erotic Wisdom: Philosophy and Intermediacy in Plato's Symposium.* Albany, NY: State University of New York Press, 2008.

Sheffield, Frisbee C. C. Introduction to *The Symposium*, by Plato, translated by M. C. Howatson, edited by M. C. Howatson and Frisbee C. C. Sheffield. Cambridge: Cambridge University Press, 2008.

Plato's Symposium: The Ethics of Desire. Oxford: Oxford University Press, 2006.

Steiner, Deborah Tarn. *Images in Mind: Statues in Archaic and Classical Greek*

Literature and Thought. Princeton, NJ: Princeton University Press, 2002.

Vlastos. Gregory. "The Individual as an Object of Love in Plato." In *Platonic Studies,* edited by Gregory Vlastos, 3–42. Princeton NJ: Princeton University Press, 1973.

Whitehead, A. N. *Process and Reality: An Essay in Cosmology*, corrected edition. New York: The Free Press, 1978.

Xenophon. *Conversations of Socrates.* Translated by Hugh Tredennick and Robin Waterfield. London: Penguin, 1990.

Zuckert, Catherine H. *Plato's Philosophers: The Coherence of the Dialogues.* Chicago: University of Chicago Press, 2009.

THE MACAT LIBRARY
BY DISCIPLINE

AFRICANA STUDIES

Chinua Achebe's *An Image of Africa: Racism in Conrad's Heart of Darkness*
W. E. B. Du Bois's *The Souls of Black Folk*
Zora Neale Huston's *Characteristics of Negro Expression*
Martin Luther King Jr's *Why We Can't Wait*
Toni Morrison's *Playing in the Dark: Whiteness in the American Literary Imagination*

ANTHROPOLOGY

Arjun Appadurai's *Modernity at Large: Cultural Dimensions of Globalisation*
Philippe Ariès's *Centuries of Childhood*
Franz Boas's *Race, Language and Culture*
Kim Chan & Renée Mauborgne's *Blue Ocean Strategy*
Jared Diamond's *Guns, Germs & Steel: the Fate of Human Societies*
Jared Diamond's *Collapse: How Societies Choose to Fail or Survive*
E. E. Evans-Pritchard's *Witchcraft, Oracles and Magic Among the Azande*
James Ferguson's *The Anti-Politics Machine*
Clifford Geertz's *The Interpretation of Cultures*
David Graeber's *Debt: the First 5000 Years*
Karen Ho's *Liquidated: An Ethnography of Wall Street*
Geert Hofstede's *Culture's Consequences: Comparing Values, Behaviors, Institutes and Organizations across Nations*
Claude Lévi-Strauss's *Structural Anthropology*
Jay Macleod's *Ain't No Makin' It: Aspirations and Attainment in a Low-Income Neighborhood*
Saba Mahmood's *The Politics of Piety: The Islamic Revival and the Feminist Subject*
Marcel Mauss's *The Gift*

BUSINESS

Jean Lave & Etienne Wenger's *Situated Learning*
Theodore Levitt's *Marketing Myopia*
Burton G. Malkiel's *A Random Walk Down Wall Street*
Douglas McGregor's *The Human Side of Enterprise*
Michael Porter's *Competitive Strategy: Creating and Sustaining Superior Performance*
John Kotter's *Leading Change*
C. K. Prahalad & Gary Hamel's *The Core Competence of the Corporation*

CRIMINOLOGY

Michelle Alexander's *The New Jim Crow: Mass Incarceration in the Age of Colorblindness*
Michael R. Gottfredson & Travis Hirschi's *A General Theory of Crime*
Richard Herrnstein & Charles A. Murray's *The Bell Curve: Intelligence and Class Structure in American Life*
Elizabeth Loftus's *Eyewitness Testimony*
Jay Macleod's *Ain't No Makin' It: Aspirations and Attainment in a Low-Income Neighborhood*
Philip Zimbardo's *The Lucifer Effect*

ECONOMICS

Janet Abu-Lughod's *Before European Hegemony*
Ha-Joon Chang's *Kicking Away the Ladder*
David Brion Davis's *The Problem of Slavery in the Age of Revolution*
Milton Friedman's *The Role of Monetary Policy*
Milton Friedman's *Capitalism and Freedom*
David Graeber's *Debt: the First 5000 Years*
Friedrich Hayek's *The Road to Serfdom*
Karen Ho's *Liquidated: An Ethnography of Wall Street*

John Maynard Keynes's *The General Theory of Employment, Interest and Money*
Charles P. Kindleberger's *Manias, Panics and Crashes*
Robert Lucas's *Why Doesn't Capital Flow from Rich to Poor Countries?*
Burton G. Malkiel's *A Random Walk Down Wall Street*
Thomas Robert Malthus's *An Essay on the Principle of Population*
Karl Marx's *Capital*
Thomas Piketty's *Capital in the Twenty-First Century*
Amartya Sen's *Development as Freedom*
Adam Smith's *The Wealth of Nations*
Nassim Nicholas Taleb's *The Black Swan: The Impact of the Highly Improbable*
Amos Tversky's & Daniel Kahneman's *Judgment under Uncertainty: Heuristics and Biases*
Mahbub Ul Haq's *Reflections on Human Development*
Max Weber's *The Protestant Ethic and the Spirit of Capitalism*

FEMINISM AND GENDER STUDIES

Judith Butler's *Gender Trouble*
Simone De Beauvoir's *The Second Sex*
Michel Foucault's *History of Sexuality*
Betty Friedan's *The Feminine Mystique*
Saba Mahmood's *The Politics of Piety: The Islamic Revival and the Feminist Subject*
Joan Wallach Scott's *Gender and the Politics of History*
Mary Wollstonecraft's *A Vindication of the Rights of Women*
Virginia Woolf's *A Room of One's Own*

GEOGRAPHY

The Brundtland Report's *Our Common Future*
Rachel Carson's *Silent Spring*
Charles Darwin's *On the Origin of Species*
James Ferguson's *The Anti-Politics Machine*
Jane Jacobs's *The Death and Life of Great American Cities*
James Lovelock's *Gaia: A New Look at Life on Earth*
Amartya Sen's *Development as Freedom*
Mathis Wackernagel & William Rees's *Our Ecological Footprint*

HISTORY

Janet Abu-Lughod's *Before European Hegemony*
Benedict Anderson's *Imagined Communities*
Bernard Bailyn's *The Ideological Origins of the American Revolution*
Hanna Batatu's *The Old Social Classes And The Revolutionary Movements Of Iraq*
Christopher Browning's *Ordinary Men: Reserve Police Batallion 101 and the Final Solution in Poland*
Edmund Burke's *Reflections on the Revolution in France*
William Cronon's *Nature's Metropolis: Chicago And The Great West*
Alfred W. Crosby's *The Columbian Exchange*
Hamid Dabashi's *Iran: A People Interrupted*
David Brion Davis's *The Problem of Slavery in the Age of Revolution*
Nathalie Zemon Davis's *The Return of Martin Guerre*
Jared Diamond's *Guns, Germs & Steel: the Fate of Human Societies*
Frank Dikotter's *Mao's Great Famine*
John W Dower's *War Without Mercy: Race And Power In The Pacific War*
W. E. B. Du Bois's *The Souls of Black Folk*
Richard J. Evans's *In Defence of History*
Lucien Febvre's *The Problem of Unbelief in the 16th Century*
Sheila Fitzpatrick's *Everyday Stalinism*

Eric Foner's *Reconstruction: America's Unfinished Revolution, 1863-1877*
Michel Foucault's *Discipline and Punish*
Michel Foucault's *History of Sexuality*
Francis Fukuyama's *The End of History and the Last Man*
John Lewis Gaddis's *We Now Know: Rethinking Cold War History*
Ernest Gellner's *Nations and Nationalism*
Eugene Genovese's *Roll, Jordan, Roll: The World the Slaves Made*
Carlo Ginzburg's *The Night Battles*
Daniel Goldhagen's *Hitler's Willing Executioners*
Jack Goldstone's *Revolution and Rebellion in the Early Modern World*
Antonio Gramsci's *The Prison Notebooks*
Alexander Hamilton, John Jay & James Madison's *The Federalist Papers*
Christopher Hill's *The World Turned Upside Down*
Carole Hillenbrand's *The Crusades: Islamic Perspectives*
Thomas Hobbes's *Leviathan*
Eric Hobsbawm's *The Age Of Revolution*
John A. Hobson's *Imperialism: A Study*
Albert Hourani's *History of the Arab Peoples*
Samuel P. Huntington's *The Clash of Civilizations and the Remaking of World Order*
C. L. R. James's *The Black Jacobins*
Tony Judt's *Postwar: A History of Europe Since 1945*
Ernst Kantorowicz's *The King's Two Bodies: A Study in Medieval Political Theology*
Paul Kennedy's *The Rise and Fall of the Great Powers*
Ian Kershaw's *The "Hitler Myth": Image and Reality in the Third Reich*
John Maynard Keynes's *The General Theory of Employment, Interest and Money*
Charles P. Kindleberger's *Manias, Panics and Crashes*
Martin Luther King Jr's *Why We Can't Wait*
Henry Kissinger's *World Order: Reflections on the Character of Nations and the Course of History*
Thomas Kuhn's *The Structure of Scientific Revolutions*
Georges Lefebvre's *The Coming of the French Revolution*
John Locke's *Two Treatises of Government*
Niccolò Machiavelli's *The Prince*
Thomas Robert Malthus's *An Essay on the Principle of Population*
Mahmood Mamdani's *Citizen and Subject: Contemporary Africa And The Legacy Of Late Colonialism*
Karl Marx's *Capital*
Stanley Milgram's *Obedience to Authority*
John Stuart Mill's *On Liberty*
Thomas Paine's *Common Sense*
Thomas Paine's *Rights of Man*
Geoffrey Parker's *Global Crisis: War, Climate Change and Catastrophe in the Seventeenth Century*
Jonathan Riley-Smith's *The First Crusade and the Idea of Crusading*
Jean-Jacques Rousseau's *The Social Contract*
Joan Wallach Scott's *Gender and the Politics of History*
Theda Skocpol's *States and Social Revolutions*
Adam Smith's *The Wealth of Nations*
Timothy Snyder's *Bloodlands: Europe Between Hitler and Stalin*
Sun Tzu's *The Art of War*
Keith Thomas's *Religion and the Decline of Magic*
Thucydides's *The History of the Peloponnesian War*
Frederick Jackson Turner's *The Significance of the Frontier in American History*
Odd Arne Westad's *The Global Cold War: Third World Interventions And The Making Of Our Times*

LITERATURE

Chinua Achebe's *An Image of Africa: Racism in Conrad's Heart of Darkness*
Roland Barthes's *Mythologies*
Homi K. Bhabha's *The Location of Culture*
Judith Butler's *Gender Trouble*
Simone De Beauvoir's *The Second Sex*
Ferdinand De Saussure's *Course in General Linguistics*
T. S. Eliot's *The Sacred Wood: Essays on Poetry and Criticism*
Zora Neale Huston's *Characteristics of Negro Expression*
Toni Morrison's *Playing in the Dark: Whiteness in the American Literary Imagination*
Edward Said's *Orientalism*
Gayatri Chakravorty Spivak's *Can the Subaltern Speak?*
Mary Wollstonecraft's *A Vindication of the Rights of Women*
Virginia Woolf's *A Room of One's Own*

PHILOSOPHY

Elizabeth Anscombe's *Modern Moral Philosophy*
Hannah Arendt's *The Human Condition*
Aristotle's *Metaphysics*
Aristotle's *Nicomachean Ethics*
Edmund Gettier's *Is Justified True Belief Knowledge?*
Georg Wilhelm Friedrich Hegel's *Phenomenology of Spirit*
David Hume's *Dialogues Concerning Natural Religion*
David Hume's *The Enquiry for Human Understanding*
Immanuel Kant's *Religion within the Boundaries of Mere Reason*
Immanuel Kant's *Critique of Pure Reason*
Søren Kierkegaard's *The Sickness Unto Death*
Søren Kierkegaard's *Fear and Trembling*
C. S. Lewis's *The Abolition of Man*
Alasdair MacIntyre's *After Virtue*
Marcus Aurelius's *Meditations*
Friedrich Nietzsche's *On the Genealogy of Morality*
Friedrich Nietzsche's *Beyond Good and Evil*
Plato's *Republic*
Plato's *Symposium*
Jean-Jacques Rousseau's *The Social Contract*
Gilbert Ryle's *The Concept of Mind*
Baruch Spinoza's *Ethics*
Sun Tzu's *The Art of War*
Ludwig Wittgenstein's *Philosophical Investigations*

POLITICS

Benedict Anderson's *Imagined Communities*
Aristotle's *Politics*
Bernard Bailyn's *The Ideological Origins of the American Revolution*
Edmund Burke's *Reflections on the Revolution in France*
John C. Calhoun's *A Disquisition on Government*
Ha-Joon Chang's *Kicking Away the Ladder*
Hamid Dabashi's *Iran: A People Interrupted*
Hamid Dabashi's *Theology of Discontent: The Ideological Foundation of the Islamic Revolution in Iran*
Robert Dahl's *Democracy and its Critics*
Robert Dahl's *Who Governs?*
David Brion Davis's *The Problem of Slavery in the Age of Revolution*

Alexis De Tocqueville's *Democracy in America*
James Ferguson's *The Anti-Politics Machine*
Frank Dikotter's *Mao's Great Famine*
Sheila Fitzpatrick's *Everyday Stalinism*
Eric Foner's *Reconstruction: America's Unfinished Revolution, 1863-1877*
Milton Friedman's *Capitalism and Freedom*
Francis Fukuyama's *The End of History and the Last Man*
John Lewis Gaddis's *We Now Know: Rethinking Cold War History*
Ernest Gellner's *Nations and Nationalism*
David Graeber's *Debt: the First 5000 Years*
Antonio Gramsci's *The Prison Notebooks*
Alexander Hamilton, John Jay & James Madison's *The Federalist Papers*
Friedrich Hayek's *The Road to Serfdom*
Christopher Hill's *The World Turned Upside Down*
Thomas Hobbes's *Leviathan*
John A. Hobson's *Imperialism: A Study*
Samuel P. Huntington's *The Clash of Civilizations and the Remaking of World Order*
Tony Judt's *Postwar: A History of Europe Since 1945*
David C. Kang's *China Rising: Peace, Power and Order in East Asia*
Paul Kennedy's *The Rise and Fall of Great Powers*
Robert Keohane's *After Hegemony*
Martin Luther King Jr.'s *Why We Can't Wait*
Henry Kissinger's *World Order: Reflections on the Character of Nations and the Course of History*
John Locke's *Two Treatises of Government*
Niccolò Machiavelli's *The Prince*
Thomas Robert Malthus's *An Essay on the Principle of Population*
Mahmood Mamdani's *Citizen and Subject: Contemporary Africa And The Legacy Of Late Colonialism*
Karl Marx's *Capital*
John Stuart Mill's *On Liberty*
John Stuart Mill's *Utilitarianism*
Hans Morgenthau's *Politics Among Nations*
Thomas Paine's *Common Sense*
Thomas Paine's *Rights of Man*
Thomas Piketty's *Capital in the Twenty-First Century*
Robert D. Putnam's *Bowling Alone*
John Rawls's *Theory of Justice*
Jean-Jacques Rousseau's *The Social Contract*
Theda Skocpol's *States and Social Revolutions*
Adam Smith's *The Wealth of Nations*
Sun Tzu's *The Art of War*
Henry David Thoreau's *Civil Disobedience*
Thucydides's *The History of the Peloponnesian War*
Kenneth Waltz's *Theory of International Politics*
Max Weber's *Politics as a Vocation*
Odd Arne Westad's *The Global Cold War: Third World Interventions And The Making Of Our Times*

POSTCOLONIAL STUDIES

Roland Barthes's *Mythologies*
Frantz Fanon's *Black Skin, White Masks*
Homi K. Bhabha's *The Location of Culture*
Gustavo Gutiérrez's *A Theology of Liberation*
Edward Said's *Orientalism*
Gayatri Chakravorty Spivak's *Can the Subaltern Speak?*

The Macat Library By Discipline

PSYCHOLOGY

Gordon Allport's *The Nature of Prejudice*
Alan Baddeley & Graham Hitch's *Aggression: A Social Learning Analysis*
Albert Bandura's *Aggression: A Social Learning Analysis*
Leon Festinger's *A Theory of Cognitive Dissonance*
Sigmund Freud's *The Interpretation of Dreams*
Betty Friedan's *The Feminine Mystique*
Michael R. Gottfredson & Travis Hirschi's *A General Theory of Crime*
Eric Hoffer's *The True Believer: Thoughts on the Nature of Mass Movements*
William James's *Principles of Psychology*
Elizabeth Loftus's *Eyewitness Testimony*
A. H. Maslow's *A Theory of Human Motivation*
Stanley Milgram's *Obedience to Authority*
Steven Pinker's *The Better Angels of Our Nature*
Oliver Sacks's *The Man Who Mistook His Wife For a Hat*
Richard Thaler & Cass Sunstein's *Nudge: Improving Decisions About Health, Wealth and Happiness*
Amos Tversky's *Judgment under Uncertainty: Heuristics and Biases*
Philip Zimbardo's *The Lucifer Effect*

SCIENCE

Rachel Carson's *Silent Spring*
William Cronon's *Nature's Metropolis: Chicago And The Great West*
Alfred W. Crosby's *The Columbian Exchange*
Charles Darwin's *On the Origin of Species*
Richard Dawkin's *The Selfish Gene*
Thomas Kuhn's *The Structure of Scientific Revolutions*
Geoffrey Parker's *Global Crisis: War, Climate Change and Catastrophe in the Seventeenth Century*
Mathis Wackernagel & William Rees's *Our Ecological Footprint*

SOCIOLOGY

Michelle Alexander's *The New Jim Crow: Mass Incarceration in the Age of Colorblindness*
Gordon Allport's *The Nature of Prejudice*
Albert Bandura's *Aggression: A Social Learning Analysis*
Hanna Batatu's *The Old Social Classes And The Revolutionary Movements Of Iraq*
Ha-Joon Chang's *Kicking Away the Ladder*
W. E. B. Du Bois's *The Souls of Black Folk*
Émile Durkheim's *On Suicide*
Frantz Fanon's *Black Skin, White Masks*
Frantz Fanon's *The Wretched of the Earth*
Eric Foner's *Reconstruction: America's Unfinished Revolution, 1863-1877*
Eugene Genovese's *Roll, Jordan, Roll: The World the Slaves Made*
Jack Goldstone's *Revolution and Rebellion in the Early Modern World*
Antonio Gramsci's *The Prison Notebooks*
Richard Herrnstein & Charles A Murray's *The Bell Curve: Intelligence and Class Structure in American Life*
Eric Hoffer's *The True Believer: Thoughts on the Nature of Mass Movements*
Jane Jacobs's *The Death and Life of Great American Cities*
Robert Lucas's *Why Doesn't Capital Flow from Rich to Poor Countries?*
Jay Macleod's *Ain't No Makin' It: Aspirations and Attainment in a Low Income Neighborhood*
Elaine May's *Homeward Bound: American Families in the Cold War Era*
Douglas McGregor's *The Human Side of Enterprise*
C. Wright Mills's *The Sociological Imagination*

Thomas Piketty's *Capital in the Twenty-First Century*
Robert D. Putman's *Bowling Alone*
David Riesman's *The Lonely Crowd: A Study of the Changing American Character*
Edward Said's *Orientalism*
Joan Wallach Scott's *Gender and the Politics of History*
Theda Skocpol's *States and Social Revolutions*
Max Weber's *The Protestant Ethic and the Spirit of Capitalism*

THEOLOGY

Augustine's *Confessions*
Benedict's *Rule of St Benedict*
Gustavo Gutiérrez's *A Theology of Liberation*
Carole Hillenbrand's *The Crusades: Islamic Perspectives*
David Hume's *Dialogues Concerning Natural Religion*
Immanuel Kant's *Religion within the Boundaries of Mere Reason*
Ernst Kantorowicz's *The King's Two Bodies: A Study in Medieval Political Theology*
Søren Kierkegaard's *The Sickness Unto Death*
C. S. Lewis's *The Abolition of Man*
Saba Mahmood's *The Politics of Piety: The Islamic Revival and the Feminist Subject*
Baruch Spinoza's *Ethics*
Keith Thomas's *Religion and the Decline of Magic*

COMING SOON

Chris Argyris's *The Individual and the Organisation*
Seyla Benhabib's *The Rights of Others*
Walter Benjamin's *The Work Of Art in the Age of Mechanical Reproduction*
John Berger's *Ways of Seeing*
Pierre Bourdieu's *Outline of a Theory of Practice*
Mary Douglas's *Purity and Danger*
Roland Dworkin's *Taking Rights Seriously*
James G. March's *Exploration and Exploitation in Organisational Learning*
Ikujiro Nonaka's *A Dynamic Theory of Organizational Knowledge Creation*
Griselda Pollock's *Vision and Difference*
Amartya Sen's *Inequality Re-Examined*
Susan Sontag's *On Photography*
Yasser Tabbaa's *The Transformation of Islamic Art*
Ludwig von Mises's *Theory of Money and Credit*

Macat Disciplines

Access the greatest ideas and thinkers across entire disciplines, including

Postcolonial Studies

Roland Barthes's *Mythologies*
Frantz Fanon's *Black Skin, White Masks*
Homi K. Bhabha's *The Location of Culture*
Gustavo Gutiérrez's *A Theology of Liberation*
Edward Said's *Orientalism*
Gayatri Chakravorty Spivak's *Can the Subaltern Speak?*

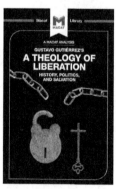

Macat analyses are available from all good bookshops and libraries.

Access hundreds of analyses through one, multimedia tool.
Join free for one month **library.macat.com**

Macat Disciplines

Access the greatest ideas and thinkers across entire disciplines, including

AFRICANA STUDIES

Chinua Achebe's *An Image of Africa: Racism in Conrad's Heart of Darkness*

W. E. B. Du Bois's *The Souls of Black Folk*

Zora Neale Hurston's *Characteristics of Negro Expression*

Martin Luther King Jr.'s *Why We Can't Wait*

Toni Morrison's *Playing in the Dark: Whiteness in the American Literary Imagination*

Macat analyses are available from all good bookshops and libraries.

Access hundreds of analyses through one, multimedia tool.
Join free for one month **library.macat.com**

Macat Disciplines

Access the greatest ideas and thinkers across entire disciplines, including

FEMINISM, GENDER AND QUEER STUDIES

Simone De Beauvoir's
The Second Sex

Michel Foucault's
History of Sexuality

Betty Friedan's
The Feminine Mystique

Saba Mahmood's
*The Politics of Piety:
The Islamic Revival and
the Feminist Subject*

Joan Wallach Scott's
*Gender and the
Politics of History*

Mary Wollstonecraft's
*A Vindication of the
Rights of Woman*

Virginia Woolf's
A Room of One's Own

Judith Butler's
Gender Trouble

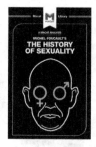

Macat Disciplines

Access the greatest ideas and thinkers across entire disciplines, including

CRIMINOLOGY

Michelle Alexander's
The New Jim Crow:
Mass Incarceration in the
Age of Colorblindness

Michael R. Gottfredson
& Travis Hirschi's
A General Theory of Crime

Elizabeth Loftus's
Eyewitness Testimony

Richard Herrnstein
& Charles A. Murray's
The Bell Curve: Intelligence and
Class Structure in American Life

Jay Macleod's
Ain't No Makin' It:
Aspirations and Attainment in a
Low-Income Neighborhood

Philip Zimbardo's
The Lucifer Effect

Macat Disciplines

Access the greatest ideas and thinkers across entire disciplines, including

INEQUALITY

Ha-Joon Chang's, *Kicking Away the Ladder*

David Graeber's, *Debt: The First 5000 Years*

Robert E. Lucas's, *Why Doesn't Capital Flow from Rich To Poor Countries?*

Thomas Piketty's, *Capital in the Twenty-First Century*

Amartya Sen's, *Inequality Re-Examined*

Mahbub Ul Haq's, *Reflections on Human Development*

Macat analyses are available from all good bookshops and libraries.

Access hundreds of analyses through one, multimedia tool.
Join free for one month **library.macat.com**

Macat Disciplines

Access the greatest ideas and thinkers across entire disciplines, including

GLOBALIZATION

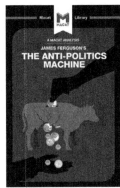

Arjun Appadurai's, *Modernity at Large: Cultural Dimensions of Globalisation*

James Ferguson's, *The Anti-Politics Machine*

Geert Hofstede's, *Culture's Consequences*

Amartya Sen's, *Development as Freedom*

Macat analyses are available from all good bookshops and libraries.

Access hundreds of analyses through one, multimedia tool.
Join free for one month **library.macat.com**

Macat Disciplines

Access the greatest ideas and thinkers across entire disciplines, including

MAN AND THE ENVIRONMENT

The Brundtland Report's, *Our Common Future*
Rachel Carson's, *Silent Spring*
James Lovelock's, *Gaia: A New Look at Life on Earth*
Mathis Wackernagel & William Rees's, *Our Ecological Footprint*

Macat analyses are available from all good bookshops and libraries.

Access hundreds of analyses through one, multimedia tool.
Join free for one month **library.macat.com**

Macat Disciplines

Access the greatest ideas and thinkers across entire disciplines, including

THE FUTURE OF DEMOCRACY

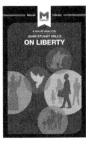

Robert A. Dahl's, *Democracy and Its Critics*
Robert A. Dahl's, *Who Governs?*
Alexis De Toqueville's, *Democracy in America*
Niccolò Machiavelli's, *The Prince*
John Stuart Mill's, *On Liberty*
Robert D. Putnam's, *Bowling Alone*
Jean-Jacques Rousseau's, *The Social Contract*
Henry David Thoreau's, *Civil Disobedience*

Macat Disciplines

Access the greatest ideas and thinkers across entire disciplines, including

TOTALITARIANISM

Sheila Fitzpatrick's, *Everyday Stalinism*
Ian Kershaw's, *The "Hitler Myth"*
Timothy Snyder's, *Bloodlands*

Macat analyses are available from all good bookshops and libraries.

Access hundreds of analyses through one, multimedia tool.
Join free for one month **library.macat.com**

Macat Pairs

Analyse historical and modern issues from opposite sides of an argument. Pairs include:

RACE AND IDENTITY

Zora Neale Hurston's
Characteristics of Negro Expression

Using material collected on anthropological expeditions to the South, Zora Neale Hurston explains how expression in African American culture in the early twentieth century departs from the art of white America. At the time, African American art was often criticized for copying white culture. For Hurston, this criticism misunderstood how art works. European tradition views art as something fixed. But Hurston describes a creative process that is alive, ever-changing, and largely improvisational. She maintains that African American art works through a process called 'mimicry'—where an imitated object or verbal pattern, for example, is reshaped and altered until it becomes something new, novel—and worthy of attention.

Frantz Fanon's
Black Skin, White Masks

Black Skin, White Masks offers a radical analysis of the psychological effects of colonization on the colonized.

Fanon witnessed the effects of colonization first hand both in his birthplace, Martinique, and again later in life when he worked as a psychiatrist in another French colony, Algeria. His text is uncompromising in form and argument. He dissects the dehumanizing effects of colonialism, arguing that it destroys the native sense of identity, forcing people to adapt to an alien set of values—including a core belief that they are inferior. This results in deep psychological trauma.

Fanon's work played a pivotal role in the civil rights movements of the 1960s.

Macat analyses are available from all good bookshops and libraries.

Access hundreds of analyses through one, multimedia tool.
Join free for one month **library.macat.com**

Printed in the United States
by Baker & Taylor Publisher Services